AMERICAN
QUILT
CLASSICS

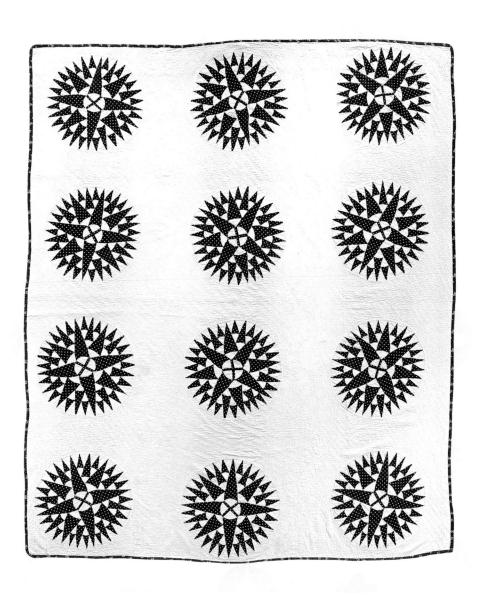

AMERICAN QUILT CLASSICS

From the collection of
Patricia Cox with
Maggi McCormick Gordon

Martingale™
& COMPANY

First published in Great Britain in 2001 by Collins & Brown Limited,
London House, Great Eastern Wharf, Parkgate Road, London SW11 4NQ

That Patchwork Place® is an imprint of Martingale & Company™.

Martingale & Company, 20205 144th Ave. NE, Woodinville, WA 98072
www.martingale-pub.com

President: Nancy J. Martin
CEO: Daniel J. Martin
Publisher: Jane Hamada
Editorial Director: Mary V. Green
Technical Editor: Karen Soltys
Designed by Alison Lee, Claire Graham
Photographer: Brent Kane
Step-by-Step Photographer: Matthew Ward

Color reproduction by Classicscan
Printed in China by DNP

06 05 04 03 02 01   6 5 4 3 2 1

> **A note on technical terms**
> Throughout this book
> technical terms that
> appear in parentheses refer
> to the UK equivalent.

Library of Congress Cataloging-in-Publication Data is available upon request

ISBN: 1-56477-358-2

> **Mission Statement**
> We are dedicated to providing quality products and service by working
> together to inspire creativity and to enrich the lives we touch.

**The quilt featured on page 1 is Mariner's Compass made in the 1890s,
the background quilt is Scherenschnitte (shown in full on page 191).
A detail from Baltimore Album is on pages 2–3 (shown in full on page 7).**

ACKNOWLEDGEMENTS
Many thanks to Barbara Chainey for putting me in touch with Maggi Gordon, and for
her friendship and belief that my quilt collection was worthy of a book about it. To
Maggi Gordon for a superb job of organizing and presenting all the information.
   Thanks to Karen O'Dowd for promoting the display of many of the quilts at the
International Quilt Festival in Houston, Texas.
   Without my favorite antique quilt dealers, Jean Lyle and Mary Koval, the collection
would not contain as many good examples as it does. Dealers Cindy Rennels, Merry
Silber and Marilyn Simmons have also been sources of some of my best quilts.
Throughout the years many students and friends and the quilt shop, Glad Creations,
where I have taught for twenty years, have led me to many other quilts.
   A very special thank-you to Meta Youngblood who for years turned many of the tops I
purchased into quilts.
   The kindness and consideration of the editors at Collins & Brown, and the photography
studio at Martingale & Company have made producing a book a painless process.
   Lastly, by not least, without my husband, Richard, I would not have been able to do all
the things I have done.

Patricia Cox

Many thanks to Patricia for allowing me to be involved in the fascinating and fulfilling
work of documenting this part of her collection, and for all her help along the way.
   To Richard Cox, too, for his wonderful hospitality, and his chauffeuring and culinary
skills while Pat and I talked quilts nonstop.
   To the team at Collins & Brown. To Matthew Ward for his patience and skill in
photographing the steps for all the projects. And to David for his on-going
encouragement and enthusiasm.

Maggi McCormick Gordon

CONTENTS

MADE FOR PAT BY HER MOTHER *c.* 1930

FOREWORD

I DID NOT START OUT to be a quilt collector. I am primarily a quiltmaker and a designer. Teaching quilting is also a high priority for me. I started quilting because the 1930s Dresden Plate quilt that my maternal grandmother gave me as a wedding present was beginning to wear out. My mother gave me a lecture on the subject of quilt care, and because of my feelings of guilt, I decided to learn how to quilt in order to replace it. I have yet to make a Dresden Plate quilt, but I have cut out the pieces for four of them and collected nine antique ones.

At the time when I began making quilts, in the mid-1960s, teachers and instruction books were not easily available. I advertised in small-town newspapers for a quilter and eventually found one in a small community in Wisconsin. She showed me the basics, and I started on my journey of discovery.

In the 1970s a number of women wanted to make quilts to celebrate the American Bicentennial in 1976. Because I had a rudimentary knowledge of quilting, I was asked to teach. And, when the National Bicentennial Quilt Show was held in Michigan in 1976, five of us drove there from Minnesota to see it. It was the first time any of us had seen so many quilts together at one time.

A few vendors were selling antique quilts at the show. One of them was Merry Silber, who had a red, green, and yellow Feathered Star quilt that I fell in love with. At the time I had only a couple of family quilts and harbored no ideas about acquiring any more, and the price of the Feathered Star was a big expenditure for me. However, at about that same time, I had started my pattern business, so I had a little extra money to spend, and I bought the quilt.

Any collector will tell you that once the fever hits, it is insidious: There is no rhyme nor reason

for it. I bought some of my quilts at house sales, some from students, but most from dealers. When I began, I did not really have a focus. I bought mostly what was available at a price I could afford and appealed to me.

Gradually, as I was asked to exhibit my quilts, I decided I had the opportunity to use the collection to educate people about the history of quilting, and about women's work. Museums usually keep their quilt collections in storage unless there is a special event, so it is difficult for most of us to have access. That is the reason I am willing to show my collection as often as I can and talk about the makers who created the quilts. As a quiltmaker myself, I feel an emotional connection to them, and when I am able to be in the presence of a really magnificent piece of work, I wish I could talk to the maker.

It was this feeling that began my adventure with Baltimore-style quilting. I am from the Midwest, so my access to Maryland quilts was limited. I had run into a few examples at quilt shows, but they had not impressed me because of their disorganized look. However, in 1980 an exhibit of about two dozen of the Baltimore Beauties had been put together by the Baltimore Art Museum, and the first place it was shown was at the Houston Museum of Fine Arts during the Houston Quilt Festival, which I was attending. The exhibit contained some of the best examples of the genre, and I stood mesmerized in front of them. The colors, the designs, the workmanship, everything about them was superlative. How I wished I could communicate with the women who designed these magnificent pieces.

Bernice Enyeart, a quilter from Indiana, had told me that she wanted to make a quilt in this style. The ones I had seen previously did not inspire me, but after viewing the spectacular

BALTIMORE ALBUM QUILT

dated 1843

The only Baltimore Album quilt in the collection is an early example with folk art patterns that have a naive quality unlike the sophistication of later quilts. In the pink wreath block above the center basket, it is dated 1843 and has the name Reisterstown, a community northwest of Baltimore. It also contains numerous signatures, including four women named Baker: Margareth in the dated block, Elizabeth in the center basket block, W.A. in the blue-jay-on-a-branch block left of the dated wreath, and Mary A.E. in the pink carnation block in the top row, second on the right. The clover block to the right of the center one is signed M.A.E. Baker, presumably also by Mary. Not all the blocks have a signature, and of those that do, some are stitched and some are stamped. Two have initials only.

exhibit in Houston, I said I would design a Baltimore-style quilt for her. It went on display at the Houston Quilt Festival in 1982, and since then I have sold patterns for this style of design and have taught people all over the world how to make this kind of quilt. It has been a labor of love.

When I had an opportunity to buy an antique Baltimore quilt, I jumped at the chance. Since the very best are priced at thousands of dollars, my finding one I could afford was a small miracle. It is an early example made before the truly great ones, but it is signed, dated, and geographically from a town located just northwest of Baltimore.

I have found that with a quilt collection, space becomes a primary consideration. Every time I begin to think about paring down the collection, someone asks me for enough pieces to mount a blue-and-white, or red-and-white, or red-and-green, or scrap, etc., quilt exhibit. So I rationalize that I can't yet get rid of the quilts I have, and maybe I can still add another one or two. And I do enjoy sharing them!

Patricia Cox

GALLERY OF QUILTS

A COLLECTION IS A PERSONAL THING. It depends upon, and reflects, various aspects of its collector, among them her interests, her eye (and that of her friends) for a bargain or an extra-special piece, her time, and of course her pocketbook. Serendipity also plays its part – gaining access to that wonderful quilt before anyone else buys it is crucial.

Over a period of time certain categories will (and do) come to the fore when a collector is thinking of adding a piece to his or her collection. It may be a particular pattern, or a combination of specific colors, or a certain time period or technique that becomes a focus for their attention. Collections almost always build up over a fairly long stretch of time, during which the collector becomes more interested in certain areas rather than others and may even shift the direction in which he or she had previously been headed.

TRADITIONAL APPLIQUÉ
VARIABLE STAR STRIPPY

The quilt pictured below is owned jointly with Pat's friend Barbara Chainey, an English quilter of great renown who spotted it at the Houston fair. As neither felt able to afford it, they purchased it together, and since Pat's quilts are American and Barbara's are British, it lives in Minneapolis, and Pat looks after it. It is Pat's oldest quilt and provides several clues to her approach to her collection. It is highly traditional, but combines its elements in ways that make it unusual. The Variable Star blocks are made from a variety of fabrics that coordinate beautifully with the fabric strips, and the workmanship is superb. The chintz strips have been cut to make full use of the pattern – even the piecing on the bottom border has been planned meticulously. After the War of 1812, chintz became widely available; the price plummeted, and quilters up and down the East Coast benefitted. Quilts such as this were one result.

c. 1825

This beautiful soft-colored quilt is the oldest in the collection. It is made as a strippy in a traditional style, widely practiced in the Northeast of England, from two documented chintz patterns, both featuring birds and printed in harmonizing colors.

COLONIAL DESIGN
THE PRESIDENT'S WREATH

c. 1840–1860

This quilt, with its extremely fine quilting and beautifully worked appliqué, is from Virginia and was never used.

The President's Wreath pattern was a popular American colonial design that was widely made, especially in red and green, as in this fabulous example, which is made from print fabrics that have lost none of their brilliance and liveliness (perhaps because the quilt was never used, so it was not exposed to the light). Absolutely typical of the late "red-and-green" era in the years leading up to the Civil War, it is an outstanding example of the quiltmaker's art.

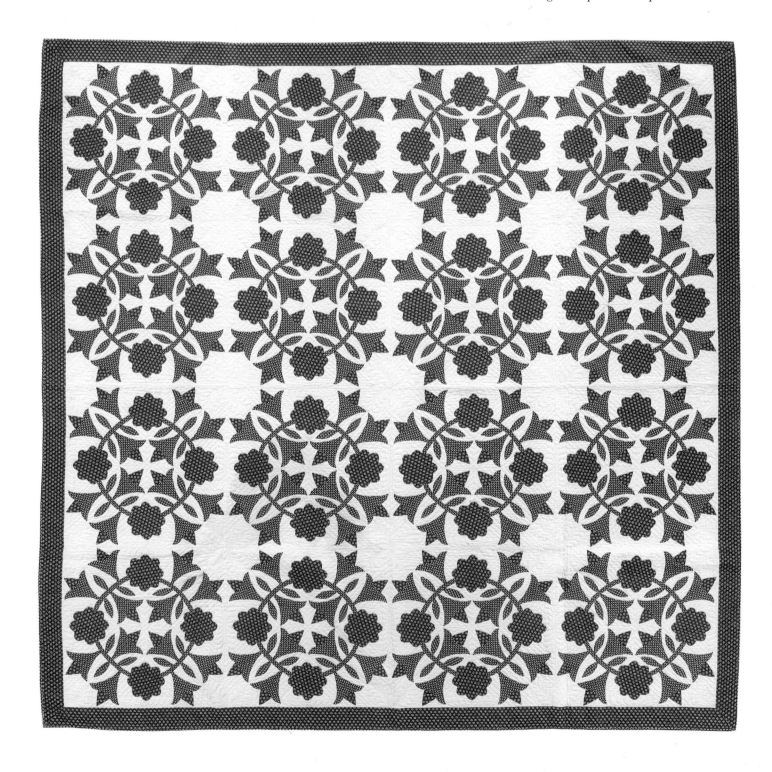

LOG CABIN VARIATION
DOUBLE-SIDED PINEAPPLE

One of the guiding principles behind Patricia Cox's collection is that her quilts should at least be unusual, and if possible, unique. This fascinating late-nineteenth-century piece is probably the latter, with two intricate and interesting quilts joined back to back to make a reversible quilt. The fabrics coordinate, from the rust color used for the edging to the heavy use of brown with blue and red. Every Pineapple block consists of light and dark brown each making up two sides of the design, with one blue and one red side. The penultimate ring is very dark brown, and the corner triangles are pieced from printed scraps that make a square between each pineapple motif. The piece is not quilted.

c. 1880

The Pineapple side of this fascinating quilt is made from wool fabric in a bold and interesting mixture of solid colors and patterns, both geometrics and prints, while the reverse, a fully usable quilt, is a more workaday mixture of wool and cotton pieced in a pattern known as Wheel of Fortune. The edge is simply turned in on both sides, and a strip of tiny triangles like prairie points is stitched between the layers.

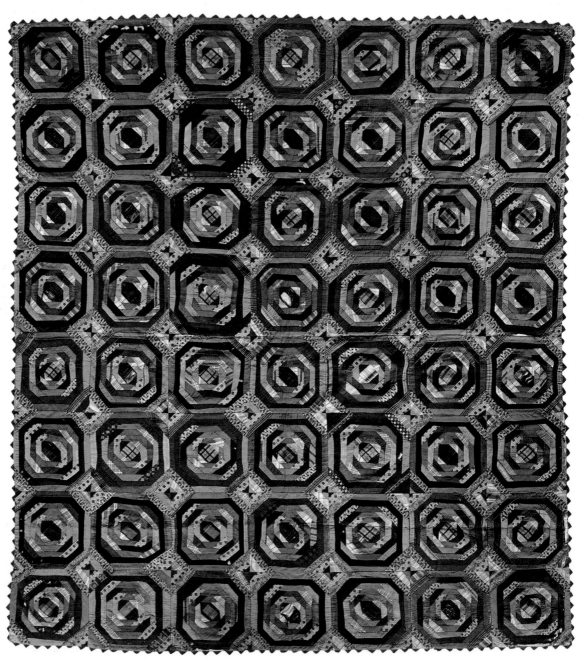

c. 1880

This traditional pattern, a sort of rectangular Trip around the World, has several possible names, including Postage Stamp, so-called because of the size of the individual pieces, which in this quilt are only 1½ inches (4 cm) square. The quilting consists of a simple horizontal and vertical grid that cuts through the diagonal of each patch of fabric.

PATCHWORK OF THE 1800s
BOSTON COMMONS

Superb workmanship is one of the most important criteria for Patricia Cox when she decides whether or not to add a quilt to her collection, so she had no difficulty with this piece on that score. It is also a glorious scrap quilt, filled with fabrics entirely typical of the late nineteenth century. The maker of this Boston Commons must have run out of material before she completed some of the rows, but most of her substitutions make sense and have been balanced with the other elements of the design. The blue border blends into the final, outer row of piecing, which consists of navy blue right-angle triangles trimmed to make a straight edge.

RED AND WHITE
REDWORK AND FRIENDSHIP QUILTS

Patricia Cox's collection contains a good selection of red-and-white quilts. These quilts were made in several different eras and cover many major design styles, and a number of them are featured elsewhere in the book. The two pictured here not only share their colors and embroidered details, but also were made at about the same time. In addition, both quilts have curved quilting that offsets and softens the rigid straight lines of the designs. However, the redwork quilt was almost certainly made by one person to be used and enjoyed for its own sake, while the friendship, or signature, quilt was a group effort, even though the individual blocks may actually have been put together by a single person.

Because Patricia Cox is very fond of the combination of red and white, she was eager to have both of these quilts for the

c. 1890

Printed embroidery motifs were sold in huge numbers in stores and by mail order, and many of them were stitched with red thread and then mounted into red-and-white quilts (like this one), which were enormously popular from the last quarter of the nineteenth century until after World War I. The designs had great charm, and some of them have been reproduced for today's quiltmakers who also enjoy embroidery.

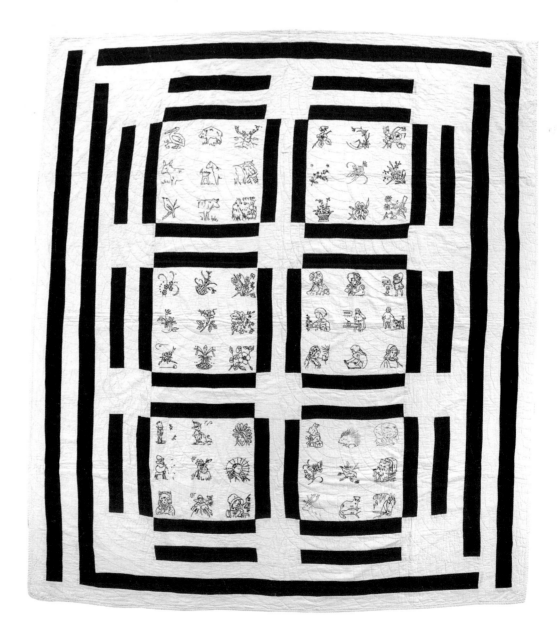

collection. The friendship or presentation quilt (below) is sometimes also known as an album quilt, but in a different sense from the Baltimore Album, and comes with a history which makes it extremely appealing. The redwork quilt opposite features many designs including a group of children of the world in national costume, another group carrying out everyday tasks, floral themes, farm and woodland animals and pets. The liveliness and variety of the embroidery motifs makes the quilt a sampler of motifs associated with redwork designs, as well as a fine example of a different sort of red-and-white quilt.

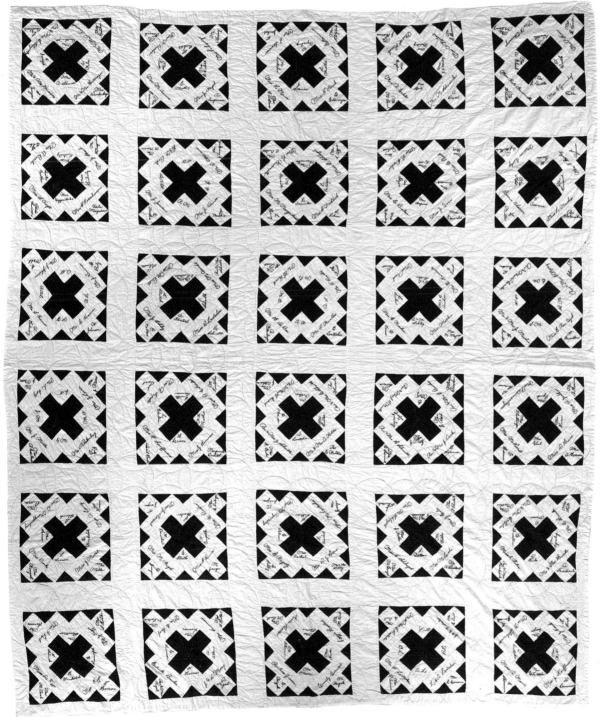

c. 1898

Before this friendship quilt came into the collection, it was owned by Lydia Schuette of Dixon, Illinois. It was made for the wife of her father, the Reverend Schuette, who was a minister in Dubuque, Iowa, possibly to raise money, perhaps for church funds or to help meet expenses in the family. The simple blocks consist of a red X in the middle surrounded by white "steps" that have been embroidered in red with the names of many people who may have paid to have their signatures included. The quilting consists of an all-over wineglass pattern.

THE GREAT WAR
RED CROSS QUILT

The Red Cross was established in 1864 by a group of nations and charitable groups to look after those wounded in war. It was finally approved in the United States in 1882, a year after a dedicated band of volunteers, notably led by the nurse Clara Barton, set up the first American branch of the organization. Barton did not live to see the horrors of World War I, but her legacy inspired quiltmakers around the country to make Red Cross quilts throughout the years when the United States participated in the conflict. The Red Cross quilts that have survived are highly collectible items, and Pat's collection is certainly enriched by this one.

c. 1915–1920

During World War I, a large number of so-called Red Cross quilts were made, usually to raise funds for the International Red Cross or to be distributed to the servicemen who might need them. Most of the quilts were distinguished by a red cross in the center. This example, with pieces the size of postage stamps, makes interesting use of myriad scraps bounded by red and white rows that act as sashing and borders.

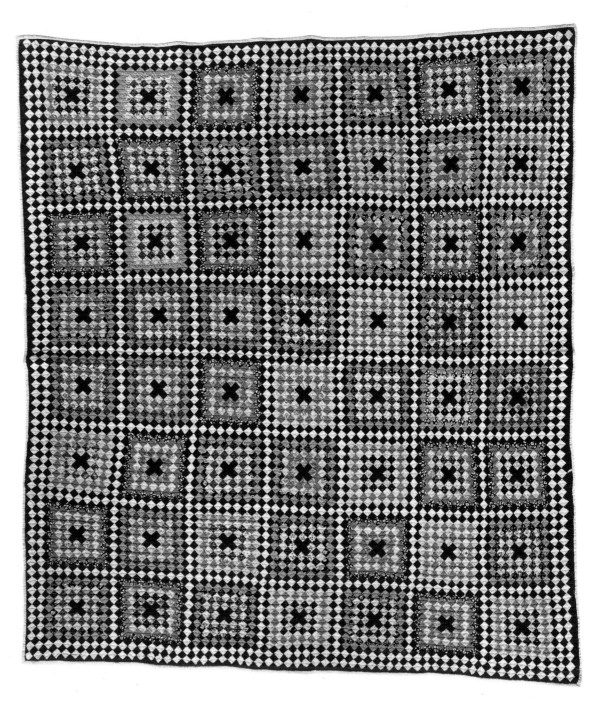

c. 1930

This whirling motif of tulips is based on a popular design by Marie D. Webster, author of the first published history of quilts and a well-known designer. But these flowers are not pieced – they are printed onto feedsacks that have been stitched together and outline-quilted with great care to give the impression of a patchwork quilt. Many quilts from this era were pieced from fabric cut from feedsacks, and larger motifs were often joined together to make backing for a quilt, but this quilt is unusual in its design and execution.

BEAUTIFUL FEEDSACKS
WINDBLOWN TULIPS

Feedsack quilts have become a collectible category, with many of the best examples finding their way into museum collections. The Cox collection has been building up over a long-enough period that a number of the quilts have a high proportion of their pieces cut from feedsacks, which were an important resource among Midwestern quiltmakers who were hit hard by the Great Depression (see pages 45–47). This piece, with its typical patchwork-type design and atypical use of whole feedsacks for the quilt top, is one of Patricia Cox's favorites.

1930s PICTORIAL PIECING
SCHOOLHOUSE

Because it is representative of an entire genre of American quilt classics, the pictorial pieced block, this Schoolhouse quilt is an important part of the collection. The Schoolhouse, one of the few pictorial blocks made by the Amish, is a popular folk-art design that dates back at least to the mid-1800s. There are many variations of the pattern, which is probably based on a stylized, and idealized, version of the rural, one-roomed little red schoolhouse of folk memory and literature. Pieced pictorial blocks were widely made in the 1930s, but Schoolhouse, baskets of all kinds, and a number of different flower and animal motifs were also worked.

c. 1930

This traditional quilt, bought in Minnesota, appealed to Patricia Cox partly for its bright colors and fine workmanship, and partly because it has some features that are unusual. Most Schoolhouse blocks, for instance, are sashed only, while on this quilt they are outlined and sashed. In addition, there is no separate outer border. The blocks, made entirely in solid-color fabrics, are outline-quilted, and the sashing has a running double-diamond pattern.

1930s SHOWCASE
Iowa Sampler

Sampler quilts, in which each block is a different pattern, have been popular and widely made since the boom in quilting classes that began in the 1980s, because they provide a showcase for the different styles of patchwork and appliqué being taught. Samplers from the 1930s, however, are fairly rare, and Patricia is delighted with this very fine example, with its interesting mix of styles and techniques, as well as its top-quality execution. The Trip around the World block, for instance, is constructed from ½ inch (1 cm) squares, combining solids and prints effectively, and the blades that make up the Dresden Plate next to it are also tiny.

c. 1930

Made in Iowa in the 1930s, this sampler quilt includes 30 different blocks made in a wide variety of typical prints and a multitude of solid colors. No single color dominates in the blocks, but the mint green sashing and the pink and green corner squares tie them together beautifully. The quilting is admirably simple: a diamond grid on the blocks, and sets of three running cable motifs along the sashing.

1930s APPLIQUÉ
MELCHIOR CASPAR BALTAZAR

c. 1930

In this unique piece worked in silk fabric, the Three Kings, or Wise Men, of the Nativity story face the viewer in their desert robes. The major technique is appliqué, but in some places the applied white fabric has been cut away to reveal the background, a once-bright blue that has faded toward gray. Their steeds seem to be horses, not the camels of the Bible, and each of the faces – animal as well as human – has a different expression. The quilting consists of a fairly large-scale diamond grid worked over the entire piece, including the borders.

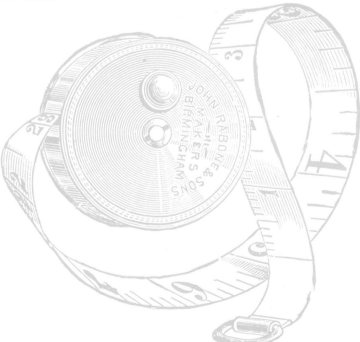

This unique piece of work was made by Miss Amelia Meckstroth, who was a somewhat eccentric quiltmaker who lived in the Chicago area. A member-by-marriage of the Sears dynasty (through her sister, who was married to a member of the family), she made a number of unusual quilts – including one featuring bats – and wall hangings.

Many of them, like this one and an exquisitely worked Madonna, were based on biblical themes. Lettering worked in appliqué was one of her passions, and one of her pieces is a beautiful rendition of The Lord's Prayer, in full, and made from silk.

She had a reputation as a strong-minded lady, and she promoted her interest in quilts by staging exhibitions of her work in her own backyard. Each of the quilts was hung on display from a clothesline – despite the threat of birds, squirrels, and the weather.

A quiltmaker all her life, Amelia left her estate to Barat College, a private institution in Lake Forest, Illinois. However her relatives succeeded in breaking her will and the college lost the bulk of the money. Amelia had issued instructions to keep the quilts together, so the college did receive them, but they subsequently sold some of the pieces to raise money. Hopefully, Miss Meckstroth would not be too unhappy to see her piece as part of this fine collection.

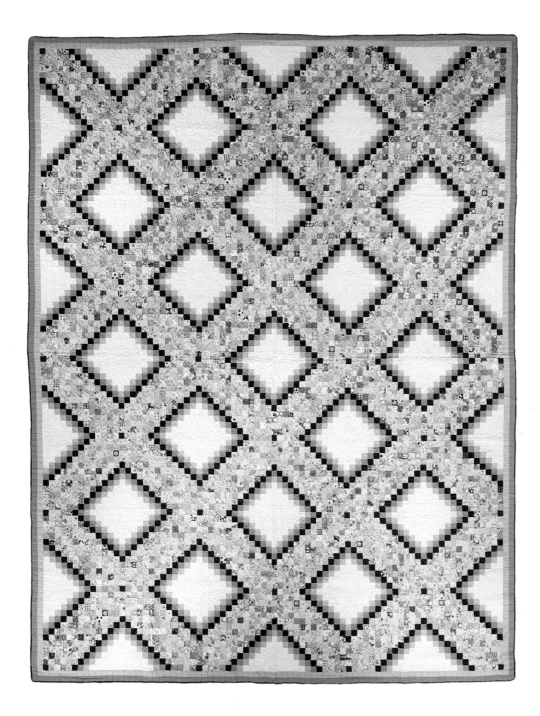

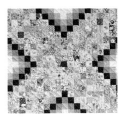

c. 1930–1940

There are actually several thousand pieces in this quintessential scrap quilt. Dozens of different fabrics, most of which are light and medium-light in value, have been used to make the 1-inch (2.5 cm) pieces. They are cleverly segregated from the white spacer blocks with three carefully planned and executed rows of green squares graduated in shade from very dark forest green to very pale. The quilting is a diamond grid on the small squares with a rose motif in each of the spacer blocks.

SCRAPS GALORE
QUILT OF A THOUSAND PIECES

This beautiful One-Patch quilt has been recorded in the Wisconsin quilt search as having been made by two sisters, and the fabrics point to a late 1930s or early 1940s date. The care with which it has been planned and put together, combined with the intricacy of the design, make it a highly collectible quilt, and it is one of the highlights of the collection. The dark outline of small squares around the spacer blocks is typical of this type of quilt in the 1930s. Notice the small red square at the center of each intersection in the diagonal chains.

1940s CURVES
TEA BAG

This intricate quilt is another of Patricia Cox's favorite scrapbag pieces. The pattern is difficult and time-consuming, with curves that are all too apt to go awry in the piecing, but it works brilliantly as a scrap quilt whose colors are arranged at random. The choice of the bold salmon pink for the border, which matches nothing but somehow goes with everything, is inspired. The white binding, slightly on the wide side, holds the piece together like a frame.

c. 1940

Many of the fabrics used in this quilt – checks, stripes, ginghams, and small-scale prints – have been used more than once, but the random way in which the sections have been combined means that they never feel repetitive. Outline quilting has been used throughout.

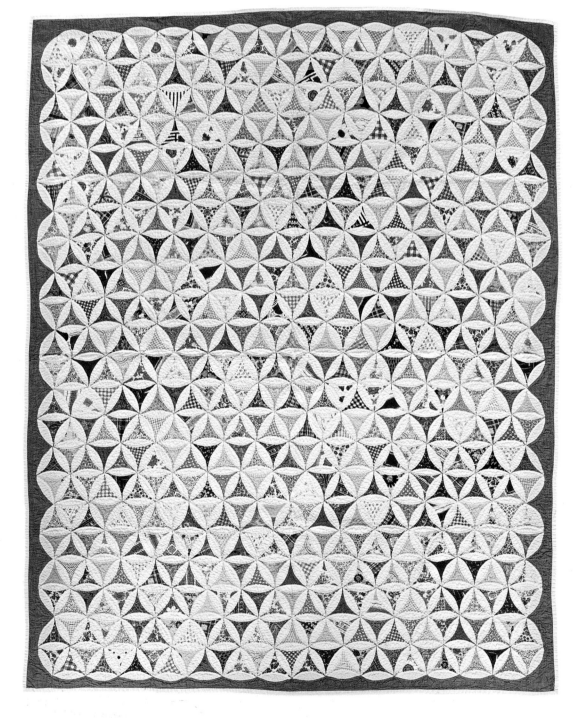

LETTERS FROM A BYGONE AGE
P FOR PATRICIA

Pat could not resist this charming, and appropriate, quilt top from Indiana, which she bought one year at the International Quilt Festival in Houston, one of her favorite shopping spots. It has a few faded, or possibly bleached, spots in some of the yellow areas, and the pink fabric used in place of the red along the left-hand edge is somewhat jarring. Also, the bottom row was badly made and caused problems when she added layers and commissioned her favorite quilter, the late Meta Youngblood, to quilt it, but she has no regrets about its purchase. A number of the fabrics, especially among the blues, appear in other quilts in the collection.

c. 1890

The numbers in the date given above are not the wrong way around, in spite of the highly graphic and modern spirit of this lively small quilt. The colors — red, yellow, and navy — and the small-scale prints on the fabrics are typical of their late-nineteenth-century origins, but they, too, have a late twentieth-century feel to them. The quilting, however, is modern.

NINETEENTH-CENTURY APPLIQUÉ

The middle years of the nineteenth century marked a high point in the making of appliqué quilts in the United States. From its beginnings as broderie perse in the late 1700s, the art of applying motifs of one color or type of fabric to a background of another developed into an American art form that was widely practiced by quiltmakers in all areas of the country.

POTS OF FLOWERS

1850–1870

This beautifully designed and executed appliqué quilt is entirely typical of its time, from the use of red, blue, yellow, and cream on a white background to the sinuous lines of the floral motifs, both in the flowerpots and in the border. It appears to have been satisfactorily well used.

ppliqué is the name given to the technique of decorating textiles by cutting out fabric shapes or motifs and applying them to a separate piece of background cloth. The method has been used in various forms and almost certainly came to North America with the earliest European settlers.

In Colonial times appliqué was used mainly on draperies and bed hangings designed to keep out drafts and the cold, and as a way to husband valuable pieces of expensive material. Cloth had to be imported into the colonies under strict laws designed to protect the great cloth-making centers in Great Britain, so even small scraps were hoarded and reused. After the Revolutionary War, spinning and

weaving moved from the home, where both had sometimes been practiced in secret to avoid severe penalties imposed by the British; and as the nation and its economy expanded in the early nineteenth century, the textile industry created domestic supplies that were within the reach of seamstresses, at least in the eastern seaboard cities.

Many textiles were still imported, however, and they were expensive, so the practice – known as "broderie perse," or Persian embroidery – of cutting motifs from patterned and extremely popular chintz cloths and applying them to plain, less expensive pieces of background fabric continued and was used on quilts as well as decorative household textiles. As fabric became more easily available and less

ROSES AND POMEGRANATES

1868

This balanced if busy design contains many typical elements, from the roses and rosebuds to the carnations that occur both singly and in pairs. Atypical, but entirely welcome, are the date, 1868, and signature that have been stitched into the background just above the paired carnations along the bottom left. The border has been carefully worked out to give the appearance, if not the actuality, of symmetry.

HARRISON ROSE

1840–1860

The Harrison Rose pattern, named for William Henry Harrison (1773–1841), the hero of the Battle of Tippecanoe and later the ninth president of the United States, can be worked as a combination of piecing and appliqué. The typical colors — red, green, and yellow on a white background — have faded slightly, but the exuberance of the design is there, with roses in two different sizes and rosebuds galore. The otherwise symmetrical border has been lost in the binding of the top left-hand corner.

expensive, and quiltmaking developed as an artistic outlet as well as a necessary part of housekeeping, appliqué became more refined, and both realistic and stylized patterns began to appear. Quilt historian Barbara Brackman also credits the mechanization of the pin-making industry, and the subsequent fall in the price of these essentials, with an advance in appliqué, since a quiltmaker who used the standard hand method to work the technique needed sharp pins in some quantity.

Some quilt historians speculate that because appliqué is more time-consuming than patchwork, appliqué quilts were most often kept for "best" and so have survived in better condition. Quilt expert Sheila Betterton, who was for many years curator of quilts at the American Museum in Bath, England (one of the finest collections in the world), has stated that she finds little evidence to support this assumption. But certainly many of the documented historical quilts that exist today were made as wedding gifts or by brides-to-be for their trousseau, and were probably treasured and especially well looked after for their sentimental attachment. At any rate, a large number of extremely fine appliqué quilts survive from the nineteenth century, including those in the Patricia Cox collection.

BALTIMORE ALBUM QUILTS

Appliqué reached its zenith between approximately 1840 and 1860 in the area in and around Baltimore, Maryland. A remarkable group of quilts of broadly similar design, unusual in many respects including

CACTUS AND COCKSCOMB

1858

This superb example of the quiltmaker's art is from Ohio. The careful planning and positioning of the motifs and the border are matched by the beautiful appliqué and the elaborate quilting. In addition to the exquisite pots of flowers quilted in the white spacer blocks, there are arcs of running feathers and highly effective triple rows of background lines behind the outline-quilted motifs.

the fact that many of them are signed and dated (a boon to quilt historians), was made. Now known as Baltimore Album quilts, they were usually worked in bright colors as blocks of fine appliqué depicting natural forms, buildings and places, stylized motifs, and even people. Most carry elaborate applied borders, and have dates and signatures of the makers written or embroidered on them. They are expensive to acquire, and most of the finest examples have found their way into museums. The only one in the Patricia Cox collection is pictured on page 7.

Many experts believe that a large number of the typical designs found on Baltimore Album quilts were devised by a small number of needlewomen, who sold them to others to be stitched. Some

examples were clearly made as group projects and show a wide diversity of sewing skill, while others were almost certainly stitched by a single highly talented individual.

MOTIFS AND DESIGNS

Meanwhile, in the rest of the country outside Baltimore, appliqué quilts were being widely worked in a huge variety of motifs. With appliqué, the curved shapes of flowers and leaves are relatively straightforward to achieve and can be worked in a more realistic way than can be accomplished in patchwork, so pictorial images abound. Sources were then, as now, all around, and pattern books, printed in large numbers and filled with designs ranging from very simple to highly elaborate and complex, were widely available.

Floral themes are everywhere. Roses appear in many forms, and the most popular, the Rose of Sharon, whose name, based on the beautiful love poem from The Song of Solomon, is found throughout the country. It has numerous variations, and was almost always, according to quilt historian Ruth E. Finlay, made as a marriage quilt. Tulips and pansies, magnolias and irises, daisies and peonies, carnations, poinsettias, thistles, and lilies occur in profusion, as do wreath shapes and leaves, from grape and mountain laurel to oak, hickory, and shamrocks. Vases, urns, and pots of flora of all shapes and sizes are found.

Birds, from peacocks to sparrows, and other animals are also depicted. Princess Feather is a popular pattern that occurs often and in a huge variety of interpretations, including a design called Maidenhair Fern.

Buildings also appear, but much less often. They are generally associated with Baltimore Album quilts, but there are some lovely pictorial quilts from the middle of the 1800s that depict churches, homes, farms, and public buildings in various ways.

Many of the designs used in appliqué were based on forms popular in folk art, much of which came to the United States with German settlers, who also employed a fold-and-cut method of creating stylized paper patterns that were used to make the motifs found on many quilts. Most of these pieces are made

SNOWFLAKE

1840–1860

This charming red-and-white quilt has a modern, graphic feel. The snowflakes, made from a small-scale printed fabric, almost certainly began life as paper cutouts, while the motifs in the border are almost abstract. The larger design (detail above) could be a bird on a limb or a horse pulling a sleigh.

ROSE OF SHARON

c. 1880

Rose of Sharon is probably the best-represented of all the rose patterns because of its association with true love and marriage. This fine example has been beautifully organized, from the planning of the twelve individual blocks to the wonderfully balanced border. The red and green fabrics are typically solid colors, except for the middle row of petals in the flowers, which are made from a red-on-red small-scale print. The seams where the blocks are joined have been quilted with a running feather; the background, including the border, is worked in a diagonal grid.

in two colors only, usually red on white or blue on white. They look somewhat like kindergarten paper snowflakes and are kin to the more elaborate and much larger Hawaiian appliqués developed by the native seamstresses, who were first taught by missionaries who settled in the islands toward the end of the nineteenth century.

COLORS AND FABRICS

The technology associated with the printing and dyeing of fabrics advanced greatly during the mid-nineteenth century. One of the most exciting developments for quiltmakers was the discovery and refinement of a colorfast bright red. Red and its associated pinks, which not only have strong graphic

Indigo was also widely used, and the era is known for its dramatic blue-and-white quilts, patchwork as well as appliqué, showing a wide variety of designs. Blue and white were the signature colors of the Temperance Society, which was at its height in the 1880s, and many blue-and-white quilts are associated with the movement.

The fabrics used for appliqué tended to be solid colors. Patterned fabrics sometimes appear, usually as small-scale prints, and geometric designs are also occasionally found.

BORDERS

The typical appliqué quilts of the mid- to late-nineteenth century, including Baltimore Albums, carry elaborate borders. Most relate to the main design of the quilt, and many consist of sinuous vines snaking around the edges of the piece with flowers, leaves, and animals worked in the same colors as those used to make the motifs. Similar highly decorative borders also occur frequently on patchwork quilts of the era, as testaments to the skills in design and technique of the makers.

POTS OF FLOWERS

1850–1870

A detail of this lovely quilt appears on pages 26–27.

qualities but also work extremely well in floral designs, became the colors of choice. They were combined with yellow and with green in myriad shades, including a sharp acid green such as the one used in the Basket quilt featured on page 162, which is virtually impossible to purchase today in order to make reproduction pieces.

PROJECT: MEXICAN ROSE
HAND APPLIQUÉ

MEXICAN ROSE

c. 1850–1860

This exquisite Mexican Rose quilt was made in the middle of the nineteenth century, probably on the East Coast, and became part of the collection in the 1980s. It is typical of its time, when red and green were widely used in quiltmaking. There are some mistakes in the small circles, perhaps deliberate "superstition" errors of the "only God can create a perfect thing" variety.

The hand-appliquéd Mexican Rose block is a challenging one – definitely not a beginner's piece. The name of the pattern commemorates the Mexican War of 1846–1848, a conflict between the United States and Mexico that was fought over disputed boundaries among other things. The war ended with the Treaty of Guadalupe Hidalgo and the acquisition of the land in 1848 that became the southwestern states.

We have marked the block on the wrong side and worked most of the flower and leaf shapes from the back. If you prefer, work from the right side as shown on pages 51 to 53.

MATERIALS FOR ONE BLOCK

1 piece of cream background fabric,
12 inches (30 cm) square

•

9 × 22 inches (23 × 56 cm) of green fabric

•

Small pieces of red and yellow fabrics

•

Thread to match appliqué fabrics

1 Trace the entire pattern on the wrong side of the background fabric. *Inset:* Then turn the fabric over and trace the stem lines for the bias strips onto the right side of the fabric.

2 Cut the green fabric into bias strips 1 inch (2.5 cm) wide. You will need to cut bias strips to a total length of approximately 48 inches (1.2 m).

3 Carefully press the bias strips in half lengthwise, wrong sides together. Make sure that you do not stretch the fabric while you are pressing it.

4 Align the raw edge of a bias strip to the marked line of a central stem on the right side of the background fabric. Use matching thread to work running stitch down the middle of the strip. Apply all central stems in this way. *Inset*: Trim raw edges close to the stitching to reduce bulk.

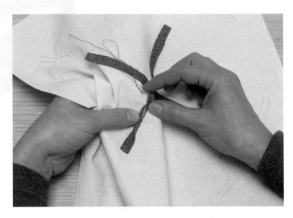

5 Turn each bias strip over to align with its opposite marked line, and blindstitch along the folded edge to secure the strips on both sides. Make sure the folded edge completely covers the raw edges.

6 Repeat for all the stems, completing the short straight lines in the corners first, then working the longer curved lines. Note that the ends of the strips will be covered by the next piece, so you do not need to turn them under.

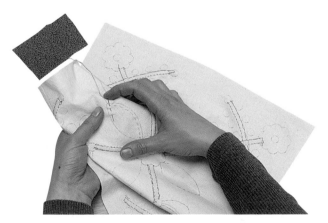

7 Cut a piece of green fabric slightly larger than the leaf shape. With the wrong side of the leaf fabric to the right side of the background fabric, work from the wrong side and baste with a contrasting thread around the inside of the shape approximately ⅛ inch (3 mm) from the marked line.

8 Turn the fabric to the right side and trim the leaf shape approximately ¼ inch (5 mm) from the line of basting. Turn the raw edge of the leaf shape under and slipstitch it in place using matching thread.

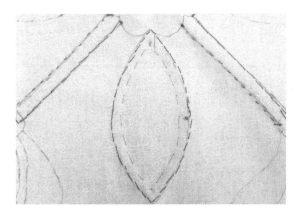

9 The stitching on the wrong side of the background fabric will follow the marked line. Appliqué all four leaves in the same way.

10 After you have appliquéd all the leaf shapes, add the red flowers in the same way. Start with the central rose and then appliqué the other roses and petal shapes. Baste, trim, and blindstitch each shape as before.

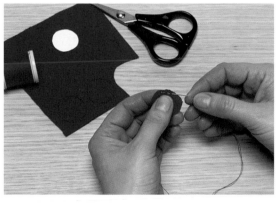

11 Using the pattern on pages 38–39, draw a small circle on the wrong side of the red fabric and cut out. Baste just inside the edge, pull up the thread tightly to make a circle, and fingerpress.

12 Whipstitch the circle in place using the same thread that was used for the basting around the edges. Repeat until you have appliquéd all the circles in the same way.

13 Repeat steps 11 and 12 to make the yellow centers and cover all raw ends of stems and petals. Remove the basting and any visible marking. Press from the wrong side only.

FINISHED BLOCK

PATTERNS

MEXICAN ROSE

One quarter of the appliqué motif is shown
on each page. To transfer the pattern you
need a sheet of paper at least 12 inches
(30 cm) square. Trace one quarter of
the pattern at a time, carefully matching
the dotted lines (center edges) as you
turn the paper to make the full pattern.

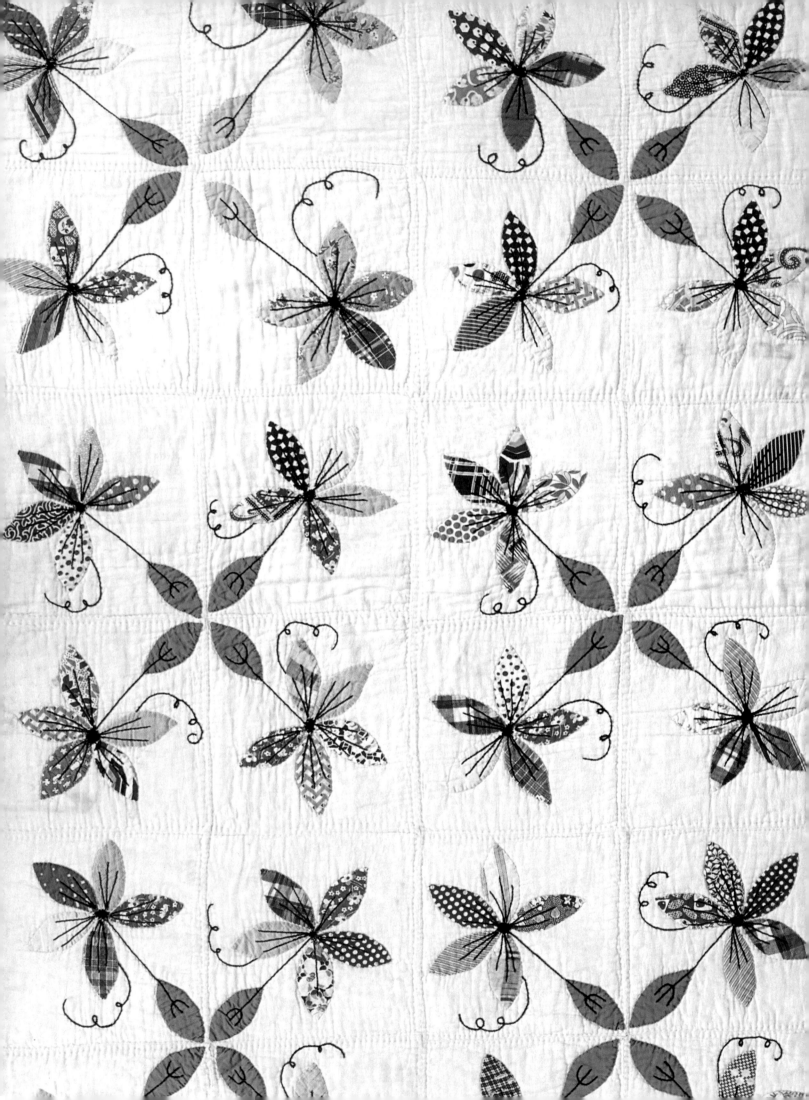

TWENTIETH-
CENTURY
APPLIQUÉ

Many of the designs of the nineteenth century, particularly the floral patterns, found their way into appliquéd quilts in the twentieth. The wide choice of plain and patterned fabrics, made more desirable by the colorfast qualities of new dyes, meant that the dark, sober hues favored by the Victorians were replaced by lively, bright pastels in a variety of styles, from Art Nouveau and Art Deco to whimsy with a capital W.

MILLIE'S QUILT

c. 1920

Designed by Millie Chaput, a talented quilter who moved to St. Paul, Minnesota, from Stone Lake, Wisconsin, this floral pattern is made in blocks. A single five-petaled flower sits in one corner joined to a single leaf in the opposite corner by a "stem" of black stem-stitch embroidery. Four blocks are joined with the leaves in the center, and the larger units are then stitched together to make the whole quilt. Each small block is outline-quilted, with diagonal rows of quilting on the pink inner and white outer borders.

Around the beginning of the twentieth century, quiltmaking in general and appliqué included, declined when machine-made woven coverlets and blankets became more widely available and less expensive than ever before. The skills were not completely lost, however. Many beautiful quilts continued to be made after the turn of the century and during the unsettling years of World War I. In the twenties, creativity roared ahead, together with good times, the economy, and women's rights. In that decade, quiltmaking moved a step away from many older traditional patterns into more free-style work. Then, when the Great Depression hit the world, people went back to needle, thread, and sewing machine to make use of what could be saved and used again. Quiltmaking flourished anew, along with dressmaking and other practical home sewing. World War II led to another decline, with entire countries involved in war work, and the postwar consumer society saw little need to make quilts when blankets and bedspreads could be acquired readymade.

From the late 1960s, small groups of dedicated quiltmakers and collectors began to halt the decline

DAFFODILS

c. 1930

Found in Grand Haven, Michigan, this lovely floral geometric design is from Stearns & Foster, one of the leading patternmakers of the day. The fabrics are all solids, with two shades of yellow for each flower and two greens for the stems and leaves. The workmanship, both of the appliqué and of the diamond grid quilting, is exquisite.

IRISES

c. 1930

Another Stearns & Foster pattern is used on this quilt, which is made, like the one opposite, with only solid-colored fabrics. Here, the leaves and stems are worked in the same color throughout, with most of the blossoms of flag iris made in two shades of a typically bright pastel. A few are worked in only one color, and two are made in yellow and mauve. This piece also is beautifully made and, with the narrow green inner and outer borders outlining a wide white one, creates the overall impression of a garden in full bloom.

of interest, and even then appliqué was very much the second-class skill to patchwork with its newfound piecing techniques. Patricia Cox was one of these rescuers, and she soon found herself at the forefront of a move to explore and advocate the practice of applied work. Then in the following decades, textile artists realized the potential of appliqué in their work, particularly in pictorial pieces, and interest was again aroused.

THE CREATIVE TWENTIES

During the 1920s, many quilts were made following traditional patterns, but there are numerous

surviving examples of original designs. Quiltmaking clearly provided a creative outlet for many stitchers, and the proliferation of patterned fabrics after World War I, which ended in 1918, made an impact on the work being done – with more to choose from, more interesting ideas could be developed. In addition, patterns galore were available from newpapers, magazines, books, and other quilters. There are a number of these quilts in the collection, several made from patterns designed and sold by Stearns & Foster, one of the best known of the companies involved in the business. In *The Romance of the Patchwork Quilt in America*, published in 1935,

ROSE OF SHARON

c. 1920

This beautiful Marie Webster design is an updated version of perhaps the most popular rose pattern of the nineteenth century. Bought in Minneapolis, Minnesota, it features roses of four layers – its precursors generally had three – put together as rings to reduce bulk. The outer ring is applied to the background, and the smaller ones are stitched in place in sequence to the center. The curvaceous three-color border with its half-open buds is worked as beautifully as the main motifs, and the wineglass overall quilting pattern makes the piece shimmer.

Carrie A. Hall and Rose G. Kretsinger declare that "Following the war, the interest was renewed, and quilt-piecing in every home from Maine to California became one of the vital interests of the day. More quilts are being pieced today in the cities and on the farms than at any previous time in the history of America, and these new ones have the charm of colonial design and meticulous handi-work." Luckily for us, many of them have been passed down and can be found in both public and private collections.

THE GREAT DEPRESSION

Many of the areas of the world that had been involved in World War I between 1914 and 1918 enjoyed some prosperity in the 1920s. The parts of Europe that had been ravaged by the fighting and by the loss of the "flower of a generation" of young men began the process of rebuilding lives and economies, while business in the United States surged ahead. Although factory wages were low and farming did not prosper during the decade, industrial production rose dramatically, urbanization increased rapidly, and the stock market boomed.

Then, on October 29, 1929, a great wave of selling stocks and shares triggered a financial crash that started on Wall Street and quickly spread around the world. The length of this depression, and its depth throughout the economy, was unprecedented, and millions of people lost everything: jobs, homes, savings. Unemployment was rife; there were no jobs to fill, and no money to buy anything but the barest necessities. Everything was eked out, reused, and then recycled – and many quiltmakers responded by creating stunning pieces of work. Patterns were still published, and old patterns were revived and reused, together with pieces of cloth left over from dressmaking and feedsacks made of cotton, which were printed in lively patterns. In spite of the level of hardship being felt throughout the country, quilts from the decade display originality and careful planning of layout and color. The numbers of surviving, and usually well-used, examples are testimony to how many must have been produced, in most cases after the chores were done.

Quilting was, in fact, big business. Articles about quilting and quilters, and patterns, were published in the leading women's magazines of the day in great profusion. The variety of fabrics, particularly cotton, available during the Depression was, according to quilt historian Carter Houck, larger than ever before, perhaps, she speculates, because "labor and manufacture were cheap," and colors, using newly developed dyes, were unique. Quilts of the period, both appliqué and patchwork, have a sparkle and brilliance that are hard to match.

In 1933, the Century of Progress World's Fair was held in Chicago, Illinois, and a quiltmaking contest was sponsored by Sears Roebuck, a company that has always been involved in textiles for the home and was then one of the major mail-order suppliers of fabric and other quilting and sewing necessities. The huge sum of $7,500 was offered as the grand prize, a fortune in the currency of the day. The response of American quilters was staggering: 25,000 quilts were submitted.

The 1930s are considered by some to be the era of the scrap or scrap-bag quilt, and there are certainly many quilts made entirely from scraps. Because many clothes were still homemade, households tended to have leftover fabric handy, and make do and mend was the order of the day. Small feedsacks lent themselves to use in scrap quilts, and as retailers

BUTTERFLIES

c. 1940

This jolly and beautifully constructed quilt has a new border made from a reproduction print very much in keeping with its original style. The butterflies have been given top wings of a typical 1940s print and lower wings and bodies of a coordinating solid color, with each piece of the appliqué turned and sewn with running stitches in black embroidery floss. The quilting is late twentieth century.

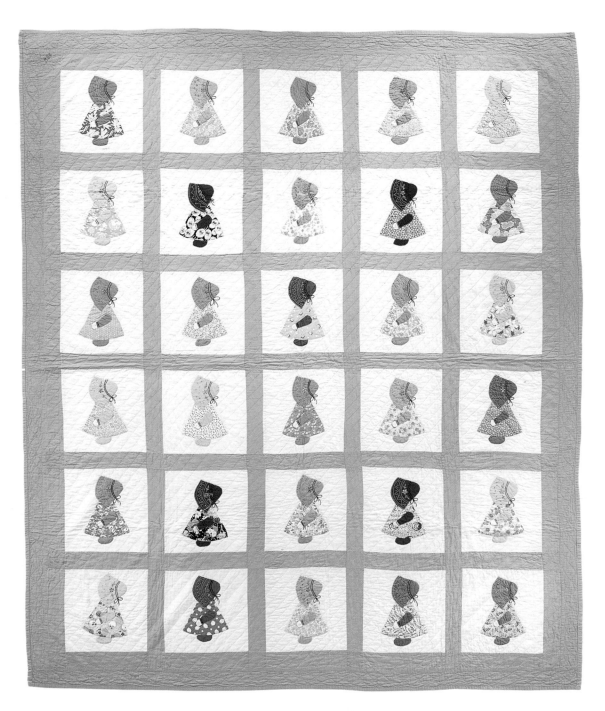

SUNBONNET SUE

c. 1930

There are many variations of this pattern, which is based on the illustrations of Kate Greenaway (1846–1901), a popular British artist known for her charming pictures of children. The boy version is called Overall Sam, and other names include Dutch Doll, Colonial Ladies, and Patricia Cox's own version, Sunbonnet Girl. Popular since the beginning of the twentieth century, this design lends itself to scrapbag work, the usual pattern being printed dresses or dungarees with solid arms, feet, and bonnets. On this typical rendering of Sue, the hat of each little girl is embroidered with the same flower, ribbon, and trim on the brim.

realized there was a market, stores and mail-order companies bundled up bags of assorted scraps from their own remnants and sold them cheaply, benefitting customer and supplier alike. These scrap bundles were particularly suitable for appliqué work, in which pieces tend to be fairly small, and many quilts were made from them. In addition, thrift was encouraged by a New Deal program headed by First Lady Eleanor Roosevelt. The program was designed to encourage traditional handicrafts, especially among women.

THE WAR YEARS AND BEYOND

After the Depression-era renaissance in quiltmaking, interest slumped. A number of factors help to explain the lack of enthusiasm. Patterns were widely available, and creativity among the quiltmakers themselves seemed to wane. Designs became somewhat repetitive and pedestrian in many cases.

In December 1941 the United States entered World War II, and life changed forever. Women, who had been entering the workplace in slowly increasing numbers since the end of World War I, suddenly found themselves doing work that had previously been reserved for men. They worked, quilters among them, in factories and medical jobs, in management jobs, and on farms. They worked shifts, brought up children alone, grieved over shared losses – and had little time to make quilts.

In addition, there were shortages of many basic items. Material was used for uniforms, tents, parachutes, and other necessities, and little was left for quiltmaking. Paper was scarce. Although food rationing for American citizens never reached the level that it did for their allies in Europe, shortages did occur, and much time and creative energy were devoted to growing food crops and cooking with limited ingredients.

After the war came a sharp economic upturn, and the skills of those who had once made quilts for practical and aesthetic reasons became dormant for nearly three decades, until the pleasures of quilting reemerged in the 1960s. However, since the main collection stops in the 1950s, that, as they say, is another story.

DESIGNS AND INFLUENCES

In the first half of the twentieth century, designs found on appliqué quilts were highly floral. Patterns that had become traditional in the nineteenth century, such as the Rose of Sharon with its romantic context, continued to be made, and the influence of the Art Nouveau movement was seen in the lines

PAPER CUTS

c. 1950

This quilt proves that the skills used in quiltmaking had not been totally lost by the mid-twentieth century. *Scherenschnitte*, or paper cuts, such as this lively example, had been popular since the mid-nineteenth century, especially those worked in blue and white, but the patterns in this quilt are more modern. The pieced sawtooth inner border is in sharp contrast to the plain outer border with its sinuous quilted vine.

and curves of fantastical forms. Nouveau gave way to Deco, and many quilt designs of the 1920s and 1930s bear its chunkier motifs.

One designer in particular influenced the change from the dark, heavy feel of Victorian designs to the lighter, more naturalistic quilts associated with the early twentieth century. Marie Dougherty Webster (1859–1956) was a well-traveled midwesterner who wrote one of the first histories of quiltmaking and whose designs, taking inspiration particularly from the European Arts and Crafts movement and her own garden, were widely published and copied in books, magazines, and newspapers.

Repeated block patterns were widely used – as always, blocks could be worked individually when time permitted and put together when enough had been finished – with whimsies such as the Crinoline Lady, and Sunbonnet Sue and all her various incarnations of both sexes, among the most popular. Fabrics were bright pastels, with a huge choice of patterns and solids in rainbow colors available.

The influence of the designers who created patterns for the kit companies that had sprung up is seen in many of the surviving quilts, with flowing images that repeat in each quadrant or in separate blocks. Flowers, leaves, and vines occur in profusion and are sometimes seen as borders in the nineteenth-century style, but borders are generally much simpler than before – straight strips of contrasting fabric that act as frames for the design within.

CHARIOT WHEEL

c. 1950

This elaborately constructed version of a traditional design is worked in solid earth colors that give it a Southwest feel. The two different stars in the center of each wheel are beautifully executed, and each motif is appliquéd with a tiny blanket stitch. The heavy marking for the quilting – wineglass in the main portion, different sizes of cables in the three borders – still shows in a number of places.

PROJECT: MILLIE'S QUILT
HAND APPLIQUÉ

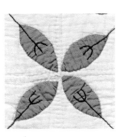

MILLIE'S QUILT

c. 1920

A great part of the charm of Millie Chaput's quilt is the varied assortment of bright pastel fabrics used to make the flower petals. Almost all of them are prints, although there are a few solid colors scattered throughout. The strong pink of the inner border provides an emphatic frame for the pattern.

Patricia Cox is probably best known for her exquisite appliqué work. She has refined her method of working to make it as simple and as neat as possible, and she teaches the technique to students worldwide. It is equally effective for large and small pieces of appliquéd work. The outline of the design is drawn lightly on the background fabric and the pieces are marked on the right side and cut out with a seam allowance. Pieces are pinned so that the line on the background fabric matches the line of the appliqué piece, and the raw edges are turned under as you work. Use a few pins, only enough to position the piece, and remove them as you get to them when you are stitching.

MATERIALS FOR ONE BLOCK

1 piece of cream background fabric,
8 inches (20 cm) square

•

Scraps of green fabrics for leaves

•

Scraps of print fabrics for petals

•

Tracing paper

•

Template plastic

•

Thread to match appliqué fabrics

•

Black embroidery floss (cotton)

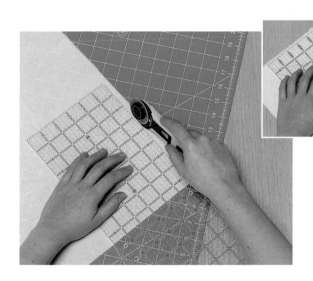

1 For each block, cut an 8-inch (20 cm) square of background fabric. Make sure the square is cut on the straight of grain. **Inset:** Mark a ¼-inch (5 mm) seam allowance on the right side all around.

2 Trace the block pattern from page 55 onto tracing paper and go over the lines with a dark marker.

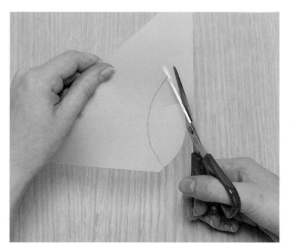

3 Trace the leaf and petal pattern on page 54 onto template plastic and carefully cut out.

4 Trace the pattern on the right side of the square of background fabric, making sure that the diagonal and straight edges line up.

5 Select the fabrics and place them right side up on a nonslip surface (for instance, a piece of sandpaper). After aligning the straight grain of the fabric very carefully, draw around the template on the right side.

6 Cut out each of the petal and leaf shapes, adding a seam allowance of approximately ¼ inch (5 mm) all around each one.

7 Some petals lie slightly behind the ones next to them. Decide which petal goes behind and pin it to the background fabric first. Do not turn the seam allowance under yet, but make sure the pins are placed through the lines drawn both on the petal pieces and on the background fabric.

8 Using thread to match the color of the petal, appliqué the shape to the background with a blindstitch. Turn under along the marked line as you stitch each piece, removing each pin as you get to it. Make sure the stitches align with the lines drawn on the background.

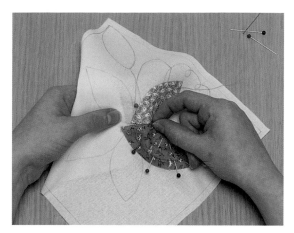

9 Keeping the stitches neat and tiny, repeat to appliqué all the petal and leaf shapes. Remember that some petals may slightly overlap one another.

10 Using the tracing made in step 2, mark the lines to be embroidered on the right side of the leaf and petal shapes. This can be done by eye, or you can use a lightbox if you have access to one.

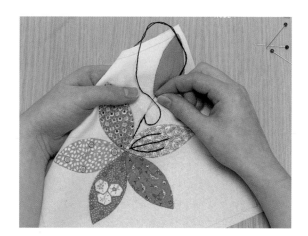

11 Using three strands of black embroidery floss, work the embroidered details with a stem stitch. The finished square can be repeated to make more blocks. Vary the petal fabrics in each block if you wish.

FINISHED BLOCK

PATTERNS

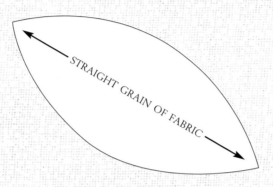

STRAIGHT GRAIN OF FABRIC

LEAF AND PETAL PATTERN

The same shape is used for both the leaf and
the petals. The pattern shown here is the
finished size. Add a ¼-inch (5 mm) seam
allowance when cutting out the fabrics.

BLOCK LAYOUT

Trace the pattern onto tracing paper and transfer it
to the right side of the square of background fabric.

STRAIGHT GRAIN OF FABRIC

STRAIGHT GRAIN OF FABRIC

KIT QUILTS

Patricia Cox has a number of kit quilts in her collection. The vogue for this type of quiltmaking was at its height mainly during the 1920s and 1930s, but kits continued to be sold – and bought in impressive numbers – through the 1950s and 1960s, and some were being made right at the end of the twentieth century. Because they were advertised nationally and sold well through mail order, strikingly similar examples can be found throughout the country. Kits were bought in the thousands. Although many of the quilts were finished, unfinished kits still turn up in attics and storerooms, and one piece in the collection is a pansy design started by Patricia Cox's mother but still not completed.

FLOWER SPRAY

c. 1940

This lovely kit quilt with its repeat patterns is simple, but made extra-special by the fabulous fan quilting, a design that echoes and enhances the shape of the appliqué motifs.

Kits for various kinds of needlework were being made in large numbers by the end of the nineteenth century after the invention of machines to stamp transferable designs onto paper and fabric. Embroidery kits and transfer patterns were popular, and so-called Penny Squares, usually embroidered with red floss, were used to make redwork quilts. Embroidery kits were also made for tablecloths and bedspreads, and soon bedcovers suitable for appliqué were also available.

By the time the United States entered World War I in 1917, kits for appliqué quilts were also being made.

Quiltmaking was growing from being a pastime based in the home, with people creating their own designs or borrowing patterns and ideas from friends and neighbors, into a big business. As a result, patterns and designs became more widespread and more standardized. Kits consisted of background fabric already printed with the overall appliqué and quilting designs; fabric – often preprinted – for

SPRING BOUQUET

*c.*1930

Lovely design touches, from the ribbon "threaded" through the fabric, to the light and dark shading of the ribbons that tie up each corner bouquet, are combined with superior workmanship to make this classic kit quilt.

making the motifs or paper patterns for making the templates; and directions for constructing the quilt. Unstamped backing fabric and sewing thread were sometimes included. Many of the designs incorporated embroidered embellishment, and those kits usually included embroidery floss as well. The background fabric was generally light-colored, almost always either white, cream, or occasionally yellow, pale green, or light blue, to make it easy to see the stamped design. The fabrics for the appliquéd motifs tended toward pastels in bright solid colors or small-scale prints. The quality of the materials was usually good, and the selling cost was astonishingly low, even by the prices of the day. Because there were few books on the subjects of appliqué and even fewer ways for a novice to learn new skills (in contrast with today, when books and classes are very much part of the discipline), kits offered beginners a seemingly simple way to make a fresh, modern-looking quilt.

PANSIES

c. 1930

In the 1930s, Patricia Cox's mother started making a twin of this kit quilt, catalog number 1365 from Paragon, and one of the most popular of all the flower appliqué kits. Pat's mother's quilt is still unfinished, so Pat added this beautifully worked finished example to her collection fairly recently to show what her mother's might have looked like.

BALTIMORE ALBUM
KIT QUILT

c. 1940

This kit is unusual in
the choice of some
patterned fabric – most
kits were supplied with
solid-colored cloth. Again,
the workmanship is
superb, and the motifs
are fresh and modern-
looking while retaining
a strong feel for its
Baltimore Album roots.
The elaborate border is
perhaps a bit heavy, but
the beautiful execution
of the carefully chosen
quilting patterns makes
this quilt a highly
collectible piece.

PATTERNS

The patterns, of which there were probably hundreds, are overwhelmingly floral, although pictorial
and novelty quilts, especially those designed for
children's rooms, were also available. The majority
of kits were for appliqué designs, although there
were kits for a number of patchwork patterns that
were particularly popular during the 1930s, such as
Double Wedding Ring, Grandmother's Fan, Lone
Star and Broken Star, and Grandmother's Flower
Garden, which may help explain the large number
of Depression-era quilts made in these designs.

The appliqué designs follow several distinctive
formats. If the stamped background fabric is square,
the same motif is often used several times. Some
quilts have four repeats, some nine, others twelve, in
regular rows; or odd numbers are set in staggered
rows that give the quilt a lively diagonal feel (as in
the detail shown on pages 56–57). On some, the
designs are different, in the style of a Baltimore
Album quilt, but the blocks are all the same size and
use the same color families. Others stagger the
repeated motifs and set them inside boxes that look
like sashing. These quilts usually have fairly elaborate

border patterns that pick up the same colors as the main motifs and are related to them in some way.

Quilts that have a large medallion-type motif in the center are often rectangular. This was the predominant shape in the 1930s, the era of the twin bed, both in Hollywood movies and in the home. The central medallion is generally either oval or rectangular, with smaller motifs surrounding the middle and usually similar but slightly different designs in the corners. Edges, particularly on kits

from the 1930s, are frequently scalloped, but most examples are likely to have plain straight sides.

Some designs have a top and bottom, and are arranged to give the quilt a definite direction. Others are mirror images at each end and on each side so it could be used with either end at the top of the bed.

MARKETING KITS

A thorough history of kit quilts has yet to be written, but Merikay Valdvogel, after extensive research, has

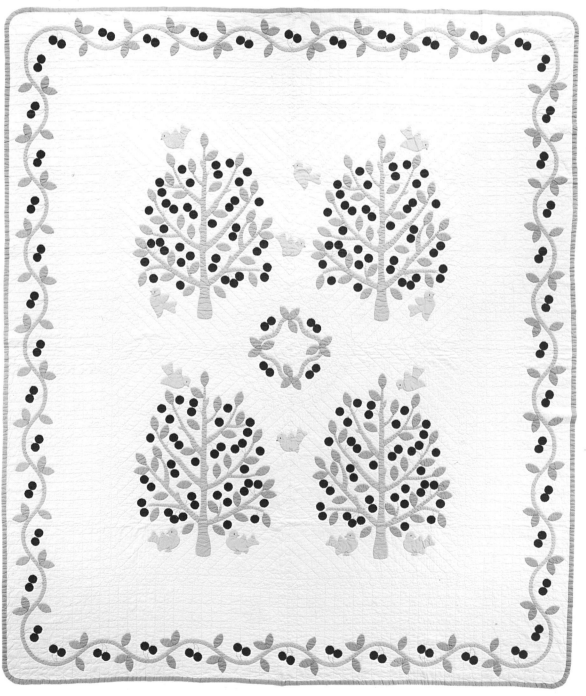

CHERRY TREES & BIRDS

c. 1920s

This is a fairly early kit quilt, a version of which was still being marketed by *Good Housekeeping* in the 1940s. Its simple balanced design of trees laden with ripe cherries being picked by three different styles of yellow birds has great charm. The quilting is similar to that on the quilt opposite, in that the central motifs are backed by one design, which is outlined with a different pattern, and the flowing border area has yet another, a simple grid.

discovered that certainly more than a dozen companies made and sold quilt kits. Among them were Paragon, Bucilla, and Progress, all of which manufactured and marketed their own kits but eventually disappeared as separate entities. The manufacturers were usually divisions of larger companies that spun thread, wove fabric, and/or printed patterns; and the catalogs of many of the smaller companies were bought and patterns reissued over a number of years, or even decades. All the needlework periodicals, and many newspapers, notably the *Kansas City Star*, and general women's magazines such as *Good Housekeeping*, regularly carried advertisements for quilt kits. Large stores and mail-order suppliers, such as Sears Roebuck and Needlework Supply Company, issued catalogs that included them.

DESIGNERS KNOWN AND UNKNOWN

As kits became more widely marketed, the manufacturers needed new designs to add to their lists. Some companies employed designers, who were (and

LACY FLOWERS

c. 1930

In her design company, One Of A Kind Quilting Designs, Patricia Cox has replicated some of the lovely motifs in this unusual white-on-blue medallion quilt as a full pattern for an appliqué quilt. The workmanship on this piece is very fine, from the all-over quilting to the dark blue embroidered flower centers.

ROSES

*c.*1930

The somewhat unusual combination of colors used in this spare appliqué pattern creates an embellishment of shading on the beautifully planned and worked background quilting, which is virtually a wholecloth quilt. The center is a spider's web, the edges of which are elaborate quilted versions of the appliqué roses. A scroll-and-feather pattern alternates with diagonal grids, some narrow, some wide, in the border area.

remain) anonymous but who were clearly trained professionals, to make patterns for embroidery projects, and some of them are likely to have added quilt design to their job descriptions. Other designs were submitted by the readers of newspapers and magazines, both unsolicited and in answer to the huge number of contests organized and financed by companies and by various publications.

Several well-known individual designers like Marie Webster (see pages 49 and 118), Anne Orr, and Rose Kretsinger began with their own small businesses and sold designs to the kit manufacturers. Marie Webster, who was among other things the author of the first history of quilts, *Quilts: Their Story and How to Make Them*, published in 1915, had a profound influence on kit quilts. Disliking the dense motifs and somber colors so beloved of stitchers and interior designers at the turn of the twentieth century, she advocated the open flowing patterns and the bright pastel colors that found their way into so many of the popular designs. Kits from the individual designers were usually sold in the form of paper patterns, and the fabric was generally bought separately from the supplier marketing the design.

CONSTRAINTS AND BOUNDARIES

Kit quilts were for many years considered simplistic and lacking in creativity. They were not designed by their makers. The same or similar patterns were worked from Miami to Seattle – in fact, the Quilters' Guild of the British Isles has documented a number of kit quilts that made their way to Great Britain. Some of these are identical, but come from different parts of the British Isles. The stamped background, which was indelible, constrained a quiltmaker who might wish to incorporate her own ideas, and the pre-printed motifs discouraged her from using different fabrics for the appliqué. For those who wished to exercise their creative muscles, the same companies that supplied kits also made patterns, and many designs that started life as quilt kits were available as

BOXED FLOWERS

c. 1930

The bright pastel colors and plain fabrics used in this quilt place it in its era, the 1930s, but the use of the appliquéd grid is unusual. It is also effective, and it allows scope for an avid quilter to work inside the plain, nonfloral areas, which are filled with large roses. Outside the boxes the quilting consists of simple diagonal lines to back the vines in each corner.

patterns that could be transferred or copied onto the maker's own choice of colors and fabrics.

However, the designs of kit quilts are usually interesting and often quite beautiful, and much of the workmanship is superb. They are interesting particularly as examples of appliqué work, and make up an important part of the Patricia Cox collection. Many types of quilts are becoming scarce, and kit quilts, finished and unfinished, have become increasing collectible in the past few years.

Predictably, prices have soared, and some collectors now buy old, unfinished kits to work themselves, for although some of the designs are still available as kits, the materials in the older versions are usually of a higher quality. In the past few years, modern kits in which the fabric, pattern, and directions are provided have been selling well, and the phenomenon of the block-of-the-month craze, both appliqué and patchwork, is akin to the popularity of kit quilts in the 1930s.

FLOWER GARDEN

c. 1930

This delightful medallion-type twin-bed quilt is also firmly associated with the 1930s, in both shape and color. The appliqués would have been fairly simple to work, but the quilting in the border area is unusually elaborate. The individual blossoms outside the medallion frame add a touch of whimsy as well as color.

PROJECT: POPPIES
HAND APPLIQUÉ

POPPIES

c. 1920

This lovely summer-weight coverlet, made from a 1920s kit, comes from Minnetonka, Minnesota. It has no batting (wadding), and when it came into the collection it was quilted with red yarn, which detracted from the superbly worked appliqué and might help to explain the bargain price that had been put upon it. Patricia Cox removed the original quilting and restitched the layers using white quilting thread in a curving quilting design typical of the kits of the day. The yellow flower centers have a green outer ring embroidered in black to look like the distinctive central area of a poppy.

Like many intricate appliqué designs, this is not a project for the beginner – or the fainthearted – but it makes a beautiful quilt in the tradition of the best of the kit quilt patterns. We have simplified the design, but the same method can be used to work the entire motif, and we have given the pattern for an interpretation of the original design on page 71.

This section shows the main middle flower of the large original design (pattern on page 70). If you break down the full design into its constituent parts, you can devise your own numbering system and work the overall design by enlarging the reduced-size diagram (page 71) and following the same method.

MATERIALS FOR ONE BLOCK

1 piece of cream background fabric, 9 inches (23 cm) square

•

Scraps of yellow and black fabrics

•

Scraps of 2 different red fabrics

•

Scraps of 2 different green fabrics

•

Template plastic

•

Green embroidery floss

1 Trace the flower design from page 70 onto the right side of the background fabric. Then trace each part of the design separately on paper or plastic and make a template for each piece.

2 Draw each piece of the design on the right side of the chosen fabric. Cut out each fabric piece, adding a generous ¼-inch (5 mm) seam allowance.

3 Write the number of each piece on the wrong side of the fabric. Make sure the numbers are correct – some pieces look similar to others.

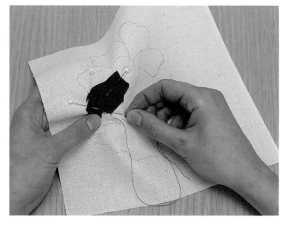

4 Pin and stitch the first piece in place. Bear in mind that any edges that will be covered by another piece do not need to be turned under or stitched.

5 Add pieces 2, 3, and 4 in order in the same way as for step 4. Make sure that you align the pins with both the marked lines.

6 Add the central circles, black first, then yellow. Draw the seamline along the bottom raw edges of the stitched pieces.

7 Add piece 7 as before. The inner edge of this petal does not need to be stitched since it will be covered by pieces 11 and 13.

8 Draw the seamlines along the inner edge of the petal as in step 6. This indicates the positioning of piece 13, the final petal. Then add the first leaf (piece 8).

9 Apply the stems one at a time. Again, because the top ends will be covered, these raw edges do not need to be turned under.

10 Pin and stitch petal 11 as before, covering the bottom raw edge of piece 7 as you work.

11 Pin and stitch the final leaf, making sure all the points are neatly turned under.

12 Add the final petal (piece 13), which will hide the remaining unstitched raw edges.

13 Mark the leaf veins to be embroidered, using a removable marker (here a white pencil). You can do this freehand by looking carefully at the diagram.

14 Work the embroidered lines in stem stitch using two strands of green embroidery floss.

FINISHED BLOCK

PATTERNS

CENTRAL POPPY

The single flower pattern is shown actual size, but can be enlarged if desired. Trace each piece separately and add a ¼-inch (5 mm) seam allowance to each fabric piece. Mark the numbers on each piece on the wrong side.

SPRAY OF POPPIES

The full design has been reduced. You can enlarge
it to 189 percent on a photocopier. Add a ¼-inch
(5 mm) seam allowance to the fabric when cutting.

LOG CABIN

Any collection of American quilts should have examples of Log Cabin, which to most people is the quintessential patchwork pattern. It combines, as no other design does, a simple construction method with literally endless variations, both within the individual blocks on which it is based and in the way in which these blocks are put together to create fascinating secondary patterns. Its infinite possibilities help to account, at least in part, for its undoubted and enduring popularity. The collection contains a large number of Log Cabin quilts, and Patricia Cox's book *The Log Cabin Workbook*, published in 1979, is based on her interest in the design.

FLYING GEESE PINEAPPLE

1875–1900

This striking Pineapple variation is made entirely of wool fabrics in an interesting variety of typically somber Victorian colors. Many of the fabrics are subtle plaids that do not enhance the contrast needed between dark and light values.

The origin of the pattern we call Log Cabin is debatable, but it probably got its name around the time of Abraham Lincoln's campaign for the presidency in 1859–1860, when much was made of his humble origins in a log house in the frontier state of Illinois. The earliest surviving American examples date from about 1860, and the pattern has been widely used throughout the country ever since.

The simple design is, however, much older. In her book *The Quilts of the British Isles* (1987), Janet Rae quotes a late nineteenth-century text that claims that cloths "covering the swathing bands of mummies, two or three thousand years old" and made the same way as Log Cabin quilts can be seen in museums in various places in Britain. Other sources claim that Log Cabin came from the West Country of England and from the Isle of Man, and the pattern is certainly found on quilts from Scotland and the North of England as well as Ireland. British examples of this type of quilt survive from the early 1800s, and descendants of Scottish settlers who went from the Hebrides to Quebec took the pattern with them and used it to make

RED-AND-WHITE, LIGHT-AND-DARK LOG CABIN

1910–1920?

This beautifully simple quilt was purchased in New England. It has no batting (wadding) and was made by stitching strips by machine to a foundation backing. Machine piecing was not widespread in the "red-and-white" period in the mid-1800s; hence the questionable date in the early twentieth century when red and white was again a popular combination. Alternating the strips is an unusual but very effective feature.

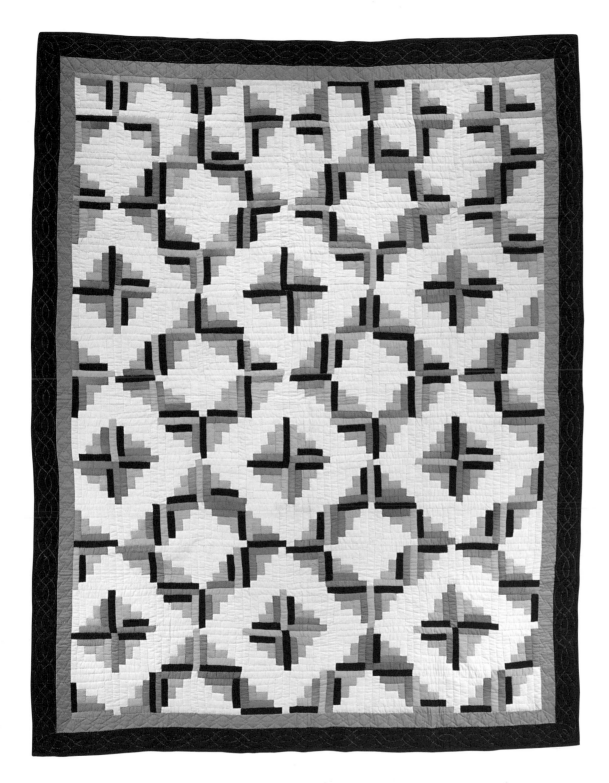

MULTICOLORED SUNSHINE AND SHADOW LOG CABIN

c. 1920

This vibrant piece, which could also be classified as a Barn Raising variation, was bought as a top in the 1980s. Because Patricia Cox believes that tops should, if possible, be quilted to prevent deterioration, she commissioned Meta Youngblood, an Iowa quilter, to complete it to give it a long life. The colorful result always, she says, makes her smile. The placement of the blocks is slightly off-center, and the top row is somewhat out of sync with the rest of the pattern.

warm bedcovers to ward off the icy blasts of the Canadian winters. Jean Dubois, in *Patchwork Quilting with Wool*, tells of Mary Morgan, an Englishwoman who emigrated to the southern states in the 1830s with a Barn Raising Log Cabin quilt, surely one of the earliest found in the United States.

Huge numbers were made in the United States during and shortly after the Civil War, and on both sides of the Atlantic during Victorian times. During the 1870s, Log Cabin quilts were so widely made that the organizing committees at various state and county fairs created specific categories for displaying and judging them.

Most of the early versions are made of wool, but as time went on, different fabrics were used, including cotton of all weights, wool challis, and then silk,

PINEAPPLE LOG CABIN

c. 1875

This wool Pineapple quilt was probably made in the Midwest, although it may have traveled west from New England. The embroidery designs in the red center squares are all different, while the simple flowers in the brown squares are all the same.

brocade, satin, and velvet, often in combination. The pattern was favored by Victorian quiltmakers, who sometimes replaced the usual strips of cloth with ribbons, which were widely used to decorate the hats, bags, and dresses worn by the middle- and upper-class women at the time.

BUILDING A LOG CABIN BLOCK

Log Cabin patchwork is worked by adding strips of cloth in a set sequence around a central square of fabric. In the standard blocks, two adjacent sides of the square are matched with light material, the other two with dark, laid, say some, one after the

other like logs in house-building. When the block was made on the Isle of Man, however, tradition says that it represented the constructing of a roof. The center square is usually red, and represents either the chimney or the hearth, the heart of the house. Some versions have dark squares, leading to speculation that the hearth had perhaps gone out in the maker's life, while others are yellow and are said to represent a lantern in the window.

There are a number of ways to construct a Log Cabin block. The oldest known method starts with a square of foundation fabric, usually muslin (calico) or homespun, on which the hearth square is centered. The technique is also called press-piecing, and early Log Cabin quilts were known as "pressed quilts." Strips are added, either by hand or by machine, around the center square in a particular order, usually two dark strips, then two light ones, or vice versa, until the desired size is reached. In some versions the strips are doubled lengthwise, with the seam sewn down the middle of the length, while others are made of one layer of fabric only, a method known today as "stitch and flip." Most early quilts on both sides of the Atlantic have been made with a foundation, but later the foundation fabric was eliminated, and strips were sewn directly to one another in strict order.

The modern method involves cutting strips and squares with rotary cutting equipment and stitching them together by machine, not onto a foundation, but by using a chain-piecing technique. The method is used universally as a way of teaching beginners the fundamentals of speed piecing in quilt-in-a-day classes, and Log Cabin is therefore one of the first quilts that many people make.

LIGHT-AND-DARK STRIP-PIECED QUILT

1880–1900

Although it lacks the central square in each block that is one of the defining characteristics of Log Cabin, this quilt is essentially, by virtue of the typical Light-and-Dark setting and its overall effect, of that ilk. Narrow strips of silk and velvet have been stitched across the diagonal of a square in which half the fabrics are light and the rest dark. Four squares combine to make each block, with the lights facing into the middle. A silk ruffle finishes the outer edge.

VARIATIONS

Varying the sequence for adding the strips of cloth changes the standard pattern: one variation is called Courthouse Steps, or White House Steps, in which strips of equal length are added on opposite sides of the center square, alternating lights and darks. The corners of the strips are stepped, giving the block its familiar names.

Strips can all be the same width, or they can be cut "thick and thin" and alternated to give a totally different effect to the finished piece. Narrow and wide strips are also used to create Asymmetrical, or Off-Center, Log Cabin. Two sides of the center square have narrow strips applied to them, and wide strips are added to the remaining two sides. The finished effect is of curving lines between blocks of light and dark, without a real curve in sight.

In Hung Center Log Cabin, the center square is turned on point. Strips are added on the square's diagonal and trimmed to make a square finished block. This method works best if it is press-pieced on a foundation square.

BLUE-AND-WHITE WINDMILL BLADES

1880–1900

The strong graphic impact of this modern-looking quilt from Ohio is enhanced by the use of plain white set against the navy-and-white patterned fabrics used for the dark sections. The number of different dark blue prints that have been incorporated is amazing, and few have been used more than once. The quilting is minimal, just enough to hold the layers together.

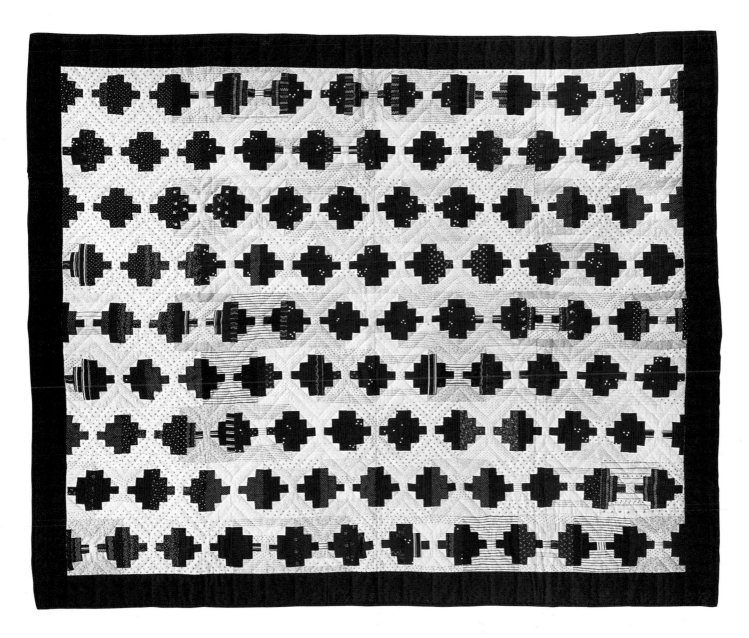

If the center square is placed in one corner of the block and strips are added to two sides instead of the usual four, the resulting Chevron or Echo Log Cabin blocks can be joined in a number of interesting patterns. A more complicated variation is Chimneys and Cornerstones, in which small squares are added to the ends of the strips to create a diagonal line of contrasting color running through each of the blocks.

The technique used to construct the basic Log Cabin block can also be used around other shapes. Triangles, diamonds, pentagons, hexagons, and irregular straight-sided pieces all work well, especially when they are worked on a foundation. Such blocks have a myriad of uses. They make good representations of flowers, and irregular shapes can form the basis for making blocks for crazy patchwork.

PINEAPPLE PATTERNS

The Pineapple variation is thought to date from the 1870s. Strips of equal width are placed around the center square, with contrasting strips at the corners stitched at an angle to produce rows of alternating triangles. The pattern must be pieced very carefully, and the planning and combining of the blocks is quite complicated, but the results can be stunning.

The pattern, which supposedly looks like the layered spiky leaves of a pineapple plant, is sometimes called Windmill Blades, as the complexity of the design gives a lively mobile effect like the spinning

RED-AND-CREAM COURTHOUSE STEPS

c. 1890

As in the quilt opposite, a wide variety of printed fabrics have been used to make a wonderfully graphic design. The backing and binding are new, and machine quilting has been worked in a diamond pattern around each block of red.

BARN RAISING
LOG CABIN

c. 1875

The center squares in
this typically Victorian
quilt are constructed
as two right-angle
triangles, one light, one
dark, which reinforces
the sharp contrast
between the concentric
rows. The bright-
colored fabrics are
silks and cottons,
and the backing is
a red plaid.

sails of a windmill. When the horizontal and vertical strips are longer than the corner ones, you have triangles that run in diagonal rows in a Flying Geese variation.

SETTING PATTERNS

The Log Cabin pattern is fascinating and infinitely variable, partly because there are so many possible ways in which the individual blocks can be configured. When the potential variety afforded by the numerous ways that blocks can be combined is added to the quiltmaking equation, there are no boundaries other than the limits of individual creativity. The blocks are joined together, edge to edge and without sashing, because any sashing

contrasting square blocks of color that form a regular pattern across the quilt.

To make a Barn Raising version (which is known in Kentucky as Light and Dark Paths), light and dark sides are set into adjacent rows so the center of the quilt is a square on point of one value surrounded by concentric rows of the opposite shading. If the color planning is carefully worked out, the color can be shaded in graduated steps, from light to dark, for example, or from one color through several stages to an entirely different color.

Straight Furrow is reminiscent of plowed fields, with blocks positioned so that diagonal lines of light sides alternate with dark ones. The blocks are usually turned with light sides touching light ones, and dark sides next to dark ones, but an interesting effect can be gained by placing all the blocks so that they face the same way, resulting in clear diagonal lines but jagged rows in between.

STRAIGHT FURROW LOG CABIN

c. 1875

The deep-red centers are less than an inch (2.5 cm) square, and there are only three rounds of strips per block. The contrasts are strong in spite of its scrappy origins. Spot the superstition block in the middle left-hand section.

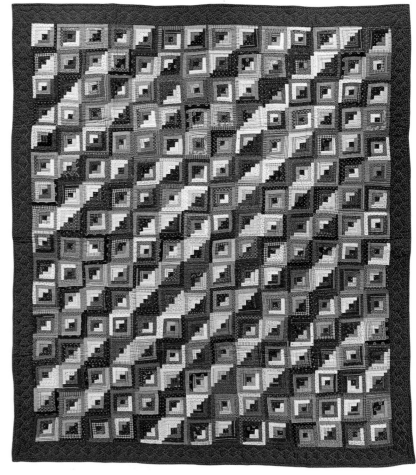

would interrupt the secondary pattern that is created by the choice of set.

There are several well-known setting patterns. One, known variously as Light and Dark, Sunshine and Shadow, and Sunshine and Shade, involves placing dark sides next to each other, and light sides adjacent in the same fashion. The result is sharply

**SUNSHINE AND
SHADOW LOG
CABIN**

c. 1890

This richly colored piece
is made entirely from
silk and velvet fabrics,
but is backed and
bound with a wholly
inappropriate cotton
paisley print. It has been
quilted by hand in
diagonal rows.

Jagged lines are also the basis of the set known as
Streak of Lightning, in which rows of light and dark are
staggered to make zigzag lines like picturebook flashes
in a stormy sky. Lazy S is a less well-known variation in
which the zigzags are set to look like the letter S
repeated throughout the quilt. Many of the variations
of the individual blocks can be arranged into any of the
settings, although some blocks work best in certain
sets, such as Light and Dark for Courthouse Steps.

FABRICS AND COLORS

Log Cabin quilts depend on strong contrasts for their
effect, not in color per se, but in their color value.
Highly successful examples can be created from a
well-endowed scrapbag, provided the colors are
sorted carefully for lights and darks. Solid colors can
also be combined beautifully, and white or cream
with a strong hue, or black or dark blue or brown
with pale colors, works particularly well.

Many patterned fabrics work as well as solid
colors, but bear in mind that prints should be small

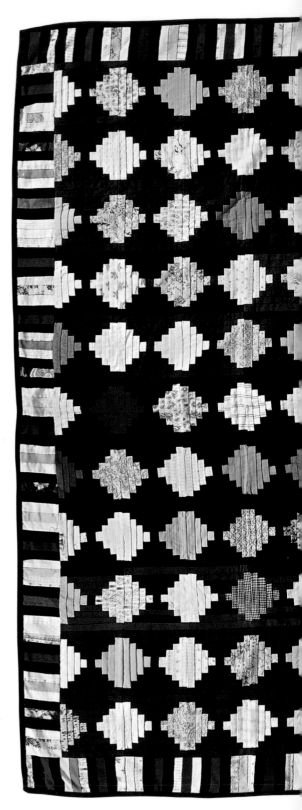

in scale, or toned harmoniously when they are cut
into strips. Otherwise, the pattern will be broken up
and the color balance may be quite inconsistent with
the chosen value. Geometric patterns such as plaids,
checks, and stripes tend to work less well since they

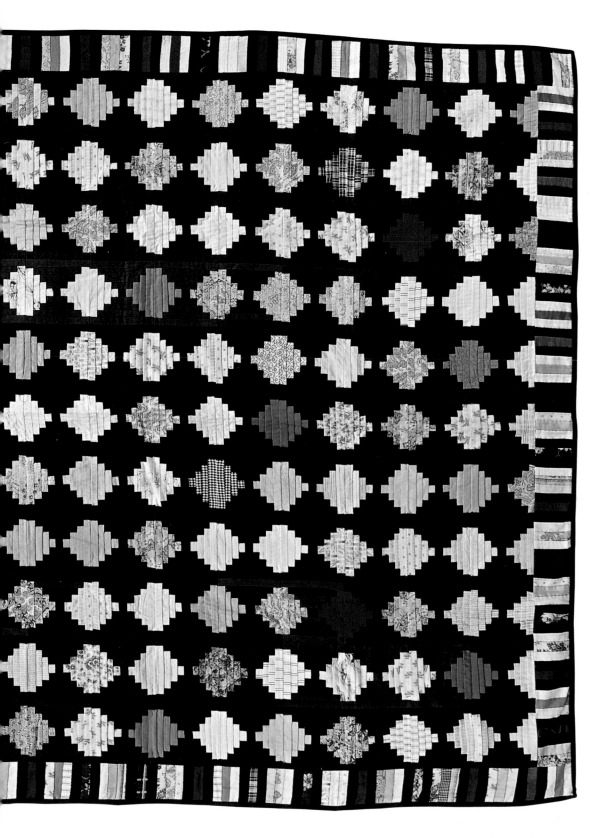

MULTICOLORED LIGHT-AND-DARK COURTHOUSE STEPS

*c.*1890

Some silk fabric has been integrated with the cottons that predominate in this late nineteenth-century quilt, and the seemingly random placement of the unusual border. It was constructed using the folded technique, in which each strip is doubled along its length and then stitched in place, making a very thick quilt. There is a tradition that if black was used for the center square in a Courthouse Steps quilt, it represented the judge's ropes.

depend themselves on color contrasts that make it hard to assign a value and may muddy the final effect.

EMBELLISHMENT

Most Log Cabin quilts have a busy feel, partly because of the profusion of pieces fundamental to the pattern, and in many cases because of the vast variety of different fabrics used to create the blocks. Embellishment would therefore perhaps seem redundant, but some of the most beautiful Log

RAINBOW BARN RAISING

1900–1920

This beautiful luminous quilt top is a "pressed" quilt. That is, it is made from strips of rainbow-colored silks that have been stitched to a foundation of muslin (calico) and arranged in concentric rows. The center squares match at least one adjacent row, which adds to the coherence of the design but creates slight indentations in certain rows. The blue watered-silk border creates an effective frame for the piece.

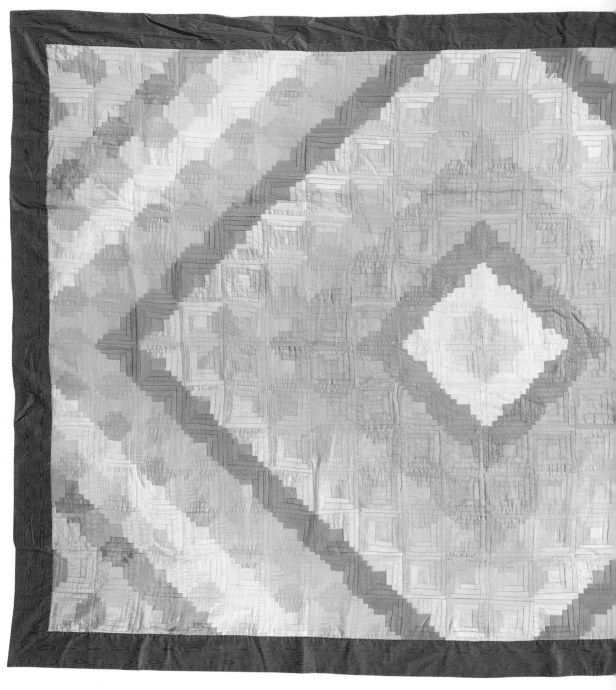

Cabin quilts have embroidered details, usually floral patterns, in the center squares. Beautifully worked Victorian examples made from silk and velvet are probably more likely than any other category to display such decoration.

BORDERS

The borders are almost always plain, usually narrow, and sometimes nonexistent. While some quilts are enhanced by the frame of a prominent border, most are happier without one, and many older quilts consist of blocks that stop at the edges of the quilt and are bound only by turning under the raw edges of the blocks and of the backing. There are, of course, exceptions, and many of them, both pieced and plain, are stunning.

Some Log Cabin quilts, particularly Victorian throws and table covers, were borderless and decorated with either gathered or pleated ruffles, or sometimes with lace or fringe, usually handmade.

QUILTING THE LAYERS

Log Cabin quilts are a mass of seams and frequently have the added bulk of a layer of foundation fabric. This means it can often be tricky deciding on a quilting pattern. Machine quilting is possible on new quilts, and hand quilting has always been very difficult to achieve. Using complex or delicate quilting patterns is usually out of the question (and any effect would be lost in the design), and many old Log Cabin quilts are simply tied and

knotted with yarn, string, or heavy thread, most often through the center square.

Hand quilting was carried out on Log Cabin quilts from the Isle of Man, in Great Britain, using an all-over pattern known as a "square wave," but most of the all-over quilting on these quilts has been done by machine, even on nineteenth-century examples. Sometimes the top layer is not quilted at all, but the batting (wadding), backing and quilt top are stitched together in some utilitarian fashion, again often by machine.

Because a lot of the surviving nineteenth-century quilts are made on foundation-fabric squares, which gives body and warmth and also adds stability, they have no batting (wadding). Many of them were used as bedspreads or summer-weight covers, while others were throws that were laid across the back of a sofa or chair, or they became table covers that could be placed over a tabletop or could protect a piano.

FLYING GEESE PINEAPPLE

1875–1900

A detail of this beautiful Pineapple variation is shown on page 72–73.

PROJECT: LOG CABIN
MACHINE PIECING

HALF LOG CABIN

1875–1900

This highly unusual Half Log, Chevron, or Echo pattern is made from a variety of fabrics typical of the era. The squares, which appear in the corner of the block, are mainly gold or red solids, but three are burgundy print. All of the "log" fabrics are prints, and the consistency of the color values is striking. Ties made from string placed in the corner of each block hold the layers together.

This is one of the simplest of all Log Cabin blocks – just remember to start each block with a light-colored strip. The color balance between the light and dark side is crucial in a pattern like this: strong color contrasts always work best.

It is possible to set the blocks together in several different ways, and it could be fun to make a number of blocks and play around with them before combining them into a larger piece.

Quilting Log Cabin quilts can be tricky because there are so many narrow seams, and many examples are tied with string as here, or with yarn or thread. Simple machine quilting is also effective.

MATERIALS FOR ONE BLOCK

1 piece of golden orange fabric,
3 inches (7.5 cm) square

•

Strips of fabric 1½ inches (4 cm) wide, half of them light-colored and half dark

•

Thread to match fabric

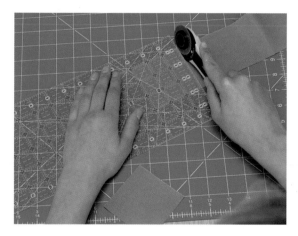

1 For each block, cut one 3-inch (7.5 cm) square of plain fabric. The original uses mainly golden orange fabrics, but mixes in red and burgundy.

2 The strips are cut 1½ inches (4 cm) wide, to finish at 1 inch (2.5 cm). Collect a selection of scraps and cut them into 1½ inch (4 cm) strips of varying length, but at least 3½ inches (9 cm). Then divide the strips into light and dark color values.

3 Using a ¼-inch (5 mm) seam throughout, stitch one light strip to a corner square, right sides together. **Inset:** Trim the strip to the same length as the square, and press the seam to one side.

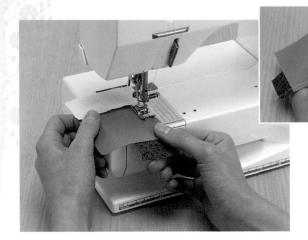

4 Placing the light strip with the corner at a right angle to the top of a dark strip, add the first dark strip.

Inset: Trim and press as in step 3.

5 Add the second light strip alongside the first. Always work with the new strip on the bottom, right side up, and place the pieced block on top of it. Trim and press as before.

6 Add the fourth strip, which should be a dark one, in the same way as before.

7 Keep adding strips, alternating light and dark. Trim each strip to the correct length and press it before adding the next. The block will build as you work.

8 Stitch the final strip – the tenth one. Then trim the block as before and press.

9 The finished block measures 7½ inches (19 cm) square. To make bigger blocks, continue adding squares. To combine blocks, put them in rows with the corner squares in the same position in each row. In the quilt shown on page 86, each row alternates the position of the squares in the next row, creating diagonal areas of light and dark. Each corner square touches the square of the block in the next row up diagonally.

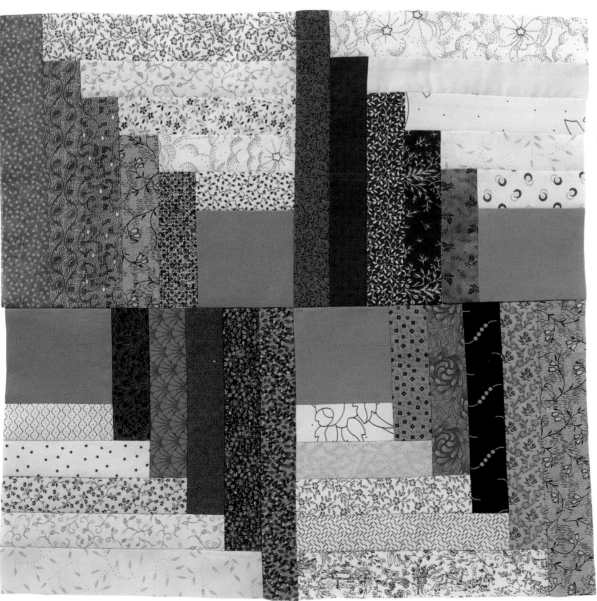

FINISHED
BLOCKS

FOUR-PATCH AND NINE-PATCH

A vast number of patchwork patterns are based on blocks known as either Four-Patch or Nine-Patch. The standard Four-Patch block is made simply by combining four units, or "patches," of fabric into a square, while the basic Nine-Patch is made from three rows of three units. Both Four-Patch and Nine-Patch designs have been used in quilts and other patchwork items since at least the eighteenth century, and the myriad variations are far too numerous to mention. Most of the standard so-called American block patterns are variations of either Four-Patch or Nine-Patch combinations, and their adaptability has meant that their appeal is widespread and perennial.

BROKEN DISHES VARIATION

1875–1900

Broken Dishes is a popular block, often made in three or more colors, which can be found in both Four-Patch and Nine-Patch versions. This variation is assembled as a square-within-a-square-within-a-square and bordered by strips made from squares and right-angle triangles. The full quilt can be seen on page 97.

The Four-Patch block is almost certainly the simplest of all patchwork to make. The most basic design is four squares joined in pairs, and the pattern relies on the contrast between light and dark color values for its overall effectiveness. The Nine-Patch, consisting in its most fundamental form of three-by-three squares, is its equal in simplicity and in versatility.

BLOCK CONSTRUCTION

The basic Four-Patch block is assembled by joining two pairs of squares that are then joined into a larger square. Four-Patch blocks can be strip-pieced by combining strips of fabric, cutting the resulting pieced fabric into strips again, and then joining the cut strips in a different order, usually with the colors reversed to make an alternating overall chessboard pattern. Different combinations of Four-Patch blocks can be joined into larger squares that make Double Four-Patch designs.

Nine-Patch blocks can also be assembled from individual squares or square units, or they can be strip-pieced using different configurations of pieced strips. In the same way that units can be combined to make Double Four-Patch blocks, nine units can be assembled into Double Nine-Patch patterns.

Simple Four-Patch or Nine-Patch blocks can be turned on point to create a lively diagonal. They can be joined in strips and used as sashing and as borders, both set square and turned on point, and they are

PINK-AND-BLUE FOUR-PATCH

1875–1900

A random collection of 552 light-and-dark Four-Patch blocks have been combined with an equal number of pink floral squares to make a quilt of great liveliness. A large proportion of the scraps are either red or brown, anchoring it firmly to the late nineteenth century, and most of the fabrics are prints. The quilting consists of straight diagonal lines, with simple fans stitched across both the inner and the outer border.

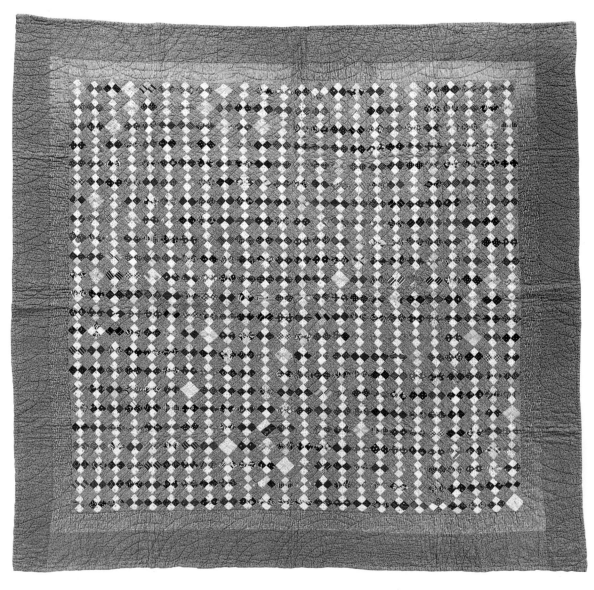

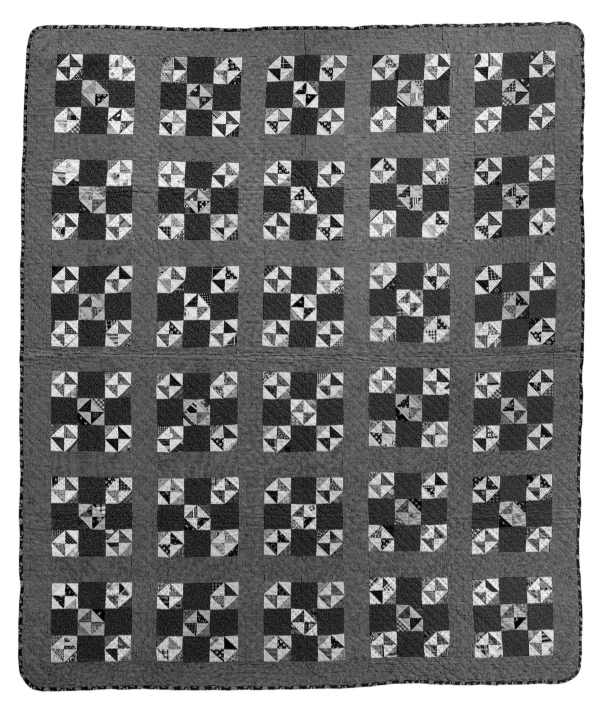

DOUBLE SQUARE

1875–1900

The large blocks are standard Nine-Patches, while the five pieced units in each one are Four-Patch in the Broken Dishes pattern. The plain squares of red and the brown sashing and border, quintessential late-nineteenth-century colors, provide a cohesive background. All the corner units are made from random prints, mainly browns and grays with a scattering of red, black, and dark blue; most, but not all, of the center units use creamy yellow as the paler color. They appear to have been placed in a carefully considered way, but they are not wholly regular – perhaps the second block in from the bottom left-hand corner is a superstition block (see page 81). The binding is a reddish-brown and tan print, and the simple quilting consists of closely spaced diagonal lines in one direction only.

often seen as corner squares in both borders and sashing. The chain effect in Single Irish Chain (see page 106) is usually created by alternating Nine-Patch blocks with plain squares of the same size across the quilt, while Four-Patch blocks can form the basis for the chain in some versions of Double Irish Chain. There are Log Cabin quilts that have simple Four-Patch or Nine-Patch blocks as the center around which the logs are placed, and blocks can be combined with strips of plain fabric in Amish Bars and Strippy quilts to great effect.

The units used to make standard Nine-Patch blocks are usually squares of the same size, but a number of patterns are assembled from units of different sizes in which the corner sections may be smaller than the central units, or the center section may be little more than strips of fabric, while the corner squares are much larger.

VARIATIONS OF BASIC BLOCKS

The units in both Four-Patch and Nine-Patch blocks can be divided into smaller squares or bars, and squares can be cut in half along the diagonal to create right-angle triangles, or set as a square within a square. These subdivisions can then be reassembled into more complex combinations that provide limitless possibilities for new patterns. Most can be strip-pieced using modern equipment and techniques that let us create beautiful machine-stitched versions, but many are part of the tradition of American block patchwork and have been worked, mainly by hand, since the early 1800s.

Many of the designs used in block patchwork were known and worked in Britain during the period when the American colonies were being settled. However, the examples that survive mainly are the borders that make up the "frames" of late-eighteenth and early-nineteenth-century quilts in Britain. These were assembled from strips of fabric surrounding a large central square or rectangle, usually made from a piece of valuable, expensive – and desirable – chintz imported from India or the East.

THE ORIGINS OF BLOCKS

When the colonists arrived in North America, they had to make do with what they had brought with

SNOWBALL

1875–1900

This beautifully graphic example of a late-nineteenth-century blue-and-white quilt is created from two very different pieced blocks. Nine-Patch blocks alternate with Snowballs in which the corner triangles are based on the size of the squares in the Nine-Patches. A number of different blue and white print fabrics have been used, and there is some variation in the white fabrics, but the Snowballs are all made from a white fabric with a tiny, regular, blue dot.

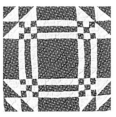

**GOOSE IN
THE POND**

1890–1910

This pattern is
sometimes called
Gentleman's Fancy, and
fancy it is. The Nine-
Patch block has all the
elements associated
with its type: squares,
bars, and triangles all
play their part in the
overall design. Here, the
white background is
actually plain white, and
the blue fabrics vary
from stripes and small-
scale motifs to dots of
various sizes. The
shades of blue differ
fairly radically, too, and
the center square of
the top right-hand
block is black. The
second block up from
the bottom right-hand
corner must be another
superstition block, or
perhaps the maker ran
out of fabric. The main
quilted area is worked
in horizontal straight
lines stitched fairly close
together, while the
quilting on the two
borders is equally
simple but worked
on the diagonal.

them, what they could grow and produce themselves, and what could be imported from the mother
countries, mainly Britain, France, Holland, and
Germany. Journeys from Europe were long and
perilous, and the price of fabric brought across the
Atlantic reflected this fact. Thrifty housewives saved
every piece of the scraps cut from dressmaking
projects, and worn-out clothes and household linen

were hoarded to be mined for the good bits that
could be cut out and used again. In addition, most
homes were small and cramped, and there was little
room to keep large sewing projects on the go.

Some of the patterns that were known lent
themselves to being assembled as blocks over a
period of time. The blocks could be stored easily
until enough had been put together to make a whole

quilt, and combining them could be done relatively quickly. When the lands beyond the Appalachian Mountains were opened up to American settlers, thousands of pioneer families went west and carried techniques and thrift with them. As the eastern seaboard became more stable and economically secure, quiltmakers could spend more time creating beautiful patterns. Myriad block patterns evolved and were given many of the names that we still use today. Among the best-known Four-Patch blocks are Pinwheel (also called Windmill), Bow Tie, Cotton Reel, Big Dipper (or Yankee Puzzle), Broken Dishes, Fox and Geese, and Birds in the Air. A number of popular star patterns, such as Evening Star and various eight-point stars, are based on Four-Patch blocks. The Nine-Patch yields at least as many versions, from Ohio Star and its large group of variations, to Shoo Fly, its cousin Churn Dash or Monkey Wrench, Jacob's Ladder, and Maple Leaf.

COLOR AND FABRIC

As with all patchwork, the choice and juxtaposition of color is the crucial element in the success or failure of a design, and Four-Patch and Nine-Patch

GOOSE TRACKS

1875–1900

This Four-Patch block is made to look more complicated by the white sashing. The planning of the design is meticulous – a different color appears in each corner of every block and joins up with three matching corners where every four blocks meet. A number of striped fabrics have also been used, each unit cut and pieced so it meets its partners to form a secondary pattern of rings linking the patches. Each piece in the patchwork has been outline-quilted, and the red-print border has a simple cable.

BROKEN DISHES VARIATION

1875–1900

It is somewhat unusual for the Broken Dishes pattern to be made in just two colors. The same blue background fabric has been used in all the plain spacer blocks in this fascinating quilt, a detail of which is shown on pages 90–91, but the blocks themselves have been made from a number of different print fabrics. They are all blue, but each fabric has a tiny white printed motif. Amazingly, they show an astonishing consistency of tone — from a distance, they could all be the same fabric. A close-spaced grid of hand-quilting covers the spacer blocks, while each unit of the pieced blocks is outline-quilted very close to the seam-line. Three plain, straight rows of stitching finish the border.

patterns are no exception. On the whole, strong contrasts work best, although many beautiful quilts exist in which the tones are muted. Historical examples of both types of patterns are frequently assembled from scraps and are not only fascinating to examine, but are also valuable research tools for the historian, especially since individual blocks may have been assembled over quite a long period of time and use fabric from several decades.

Printed fabric and solids can be used ·together in endless combinations. Among the most striking of quilts to modern eyes are the ones made from just two colors – often blue and white or red and white. The darker fabric in many of these quilts is not a solid, but strongly colored prints that display more visual texture than a solid color, and different fabrics in the same color range, can be combined to give fabulous gradations of tone and shade. Multicolored blocks can be arranged in a random fashion to create lively quilts with a country look.

Blocks can be set side by side or sashed to separate them. Spacer blocks, unpieced squares of the same size as the pieced blocks, can be used, which means that the quiltmaker needs fewer of the more intricate Four-Patch or Nine-Patch blocks to make a quilt. Most Four-Patch and Nine-Patch sets need a border or two to contain them, and these can be simple or elaborate.

PROJECT: HOURGLASS
SPEED PIECING

HOURGLASS

c. 1875–1900

This simple Four-Patch pattern has a variety of names, Double Pinwheel, Yankee Puzzle, and Big Dipper among them. The consistency of color – bright red and navy blue – is maintained effectively in spite of the use of a number of different prints of both. The quilting is finely worked: a simple cable decorates the borders, and the individual pieces in each unit of the blocks have been outline-quilted. On the sashing, rows of flying-geese triangles start in the center of the block and point toward the corners, where they meet to form Xs. Because this block is fairly easy to construct and can be done with speed-piecing methods, it is still popular today.

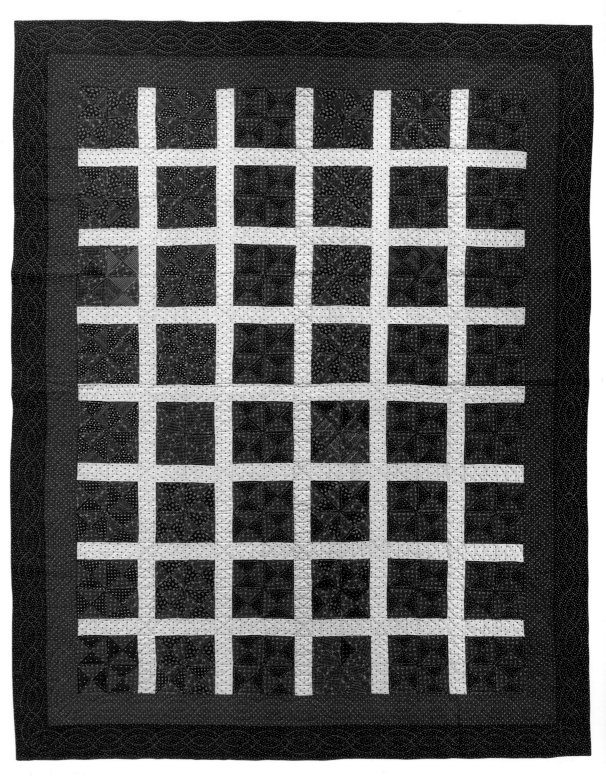

The design for this lively pattern is based on quarter-square triangles, which are made using a quick method. One square of each color yields two 4-inch (10 cm) finished pieced squares. Since triangular pieces of necessity have at least one bias seam, the method used here minimizes the tendency of any bias seam to stretch during stitching.

Measuring the size of the square is simple: to the desired finished size of the square, add ⅞ inch (2 cm) if you are cutting the square in half once (see Cakestand project page 162), or 1¼ inches (3 cm) if you are cutting twice, as in this pattern.

This method is extremely useful for making any pattern based on quarter-square triangles.

MATERIALS FOR ONE BLOCK

1 piece of red fabric, 12 inches (30 cm) square

•

1 piece of blue fabric, 12 inches (30 cm) square

•

⅛ yard (15 cm) of patterned cream fabric

•

Thread to blend

1 For each Double Four-Patch block, cut two 5½-inch (14 cm) squares of each color. If you are making a large piece, you can of course cut 5½-inch (14 cm) strips and cut the squares from them.

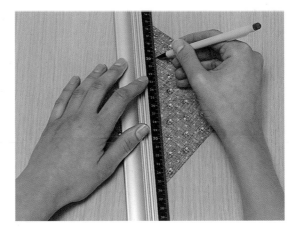

2 On the wrong side of every square of the lighter color (here red), mark a fine diagonal line from corner to corner in both directions using a pencil or fine-point marker.

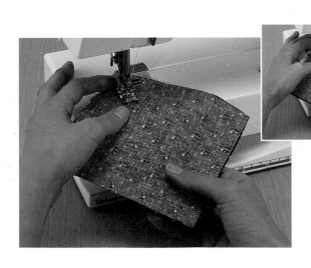

3 Place a marked light square right sides together with a dark one. Stitch a line ¼ inch (5 mm) away from one of the diagonal lines. *Inset:* Repeat on the other side of the marked diagonal line. Repeat for all squares.

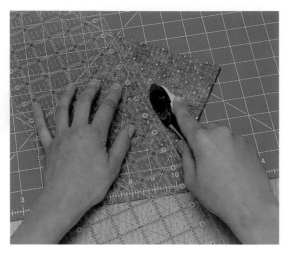

4 Cut along the diagonal line between the two lines of stitching. Press the squares with both seams toward the dark color.

5 Extend the line marked on the wrong side of the light fabric along the diagonal to the dark half of each pieced square.

6 Place two pieced squares right sides together with the red sides facing the blue ones, and stitch a double seam ¼ inch (5 mm) away from both sides of the marked line as in step 3. **Inset:** Cut along the marked line as before and press open. You need four of these pieced squares for each block.

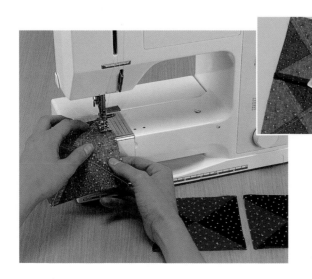

7 Arrange the pieced squares with the colors alternating, and join them in pairs.
Inset: Press the seams to one side.

8 Join the pairs into a Four-Patch block, making sure the color sequence is correct. Pin the squares together, matching the points of the triangles where they meet at the seam lines. Stitch and press.

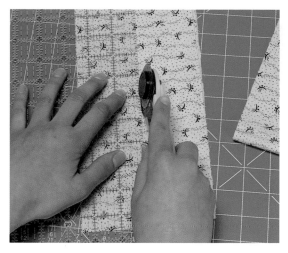

9 From the cream fabric cut strips 2½ inches (6.5 cm) wide for the sashing.

10 Join a short sashing strip to one side of each block. Press the seam toward the sashing.

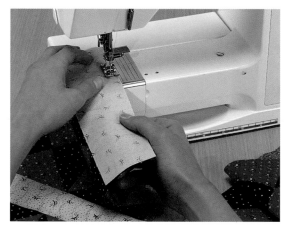

11 Join the sashed pieces together and add a final sashing strip to the unsashed side. Press.

12 Finally, add a sashing strip to each long side of the rectangle.

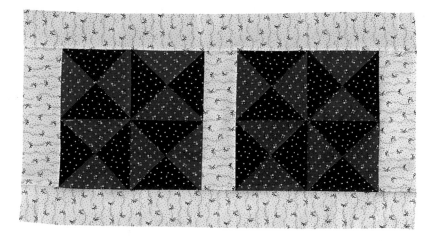

FINISHED BLOCKS

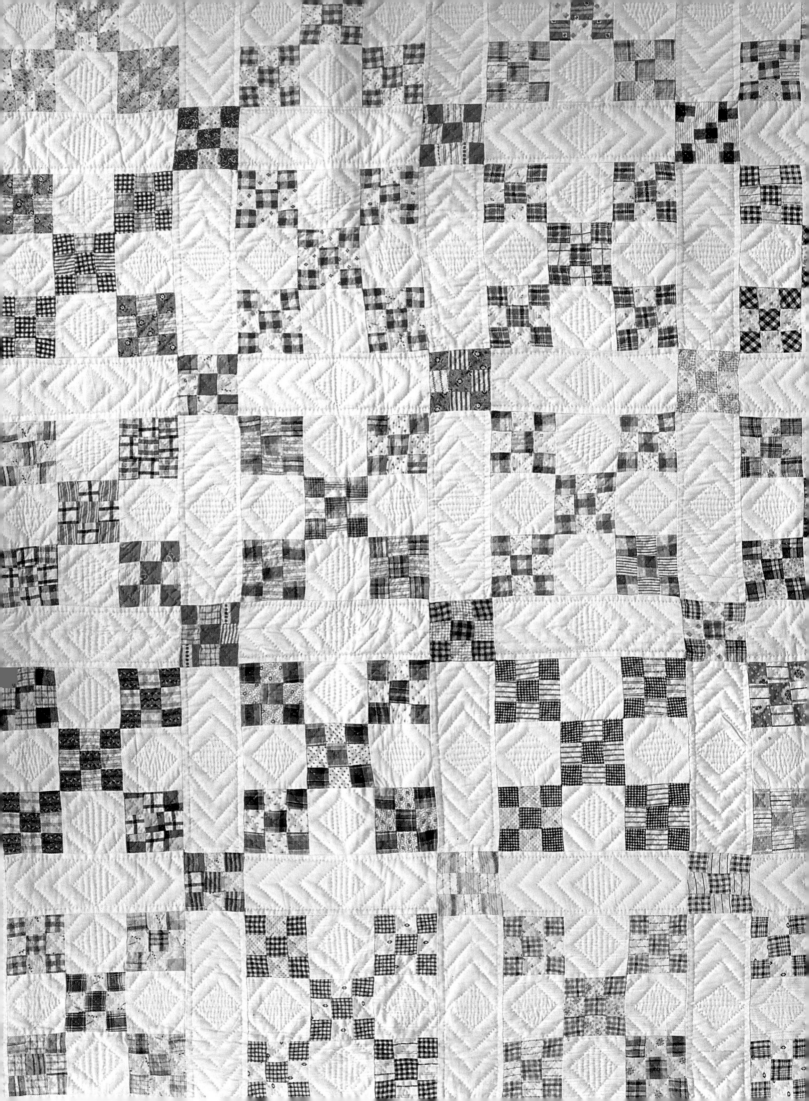

IRISH CHAIN

The origins have been lost, but the popularity of the various forms of the Irish Chain pattern does not appear to have waned since the eighteenth century. Irish Chain quilts have been found on both sides of the Atlantic for well over two hundred years and continue to be made to this day. There seems to be no evidence whatsoever that the pattern originated in Ireland, and in fact, in that island nation the design is sometimes called the American Chain.

SINGLE IRISH CHAIN

1875–1900

This beautifully conceived and executed quilt is actually a Nine-Patch Chain constructed from 1-inch (2.5 cm) squares and joined by plain white sashing strips with a single square at each corner. The chain blocks are mainly plaid, checked, and striped shirt material, although there are a few patterned fabrics, probably also shirting, interspersed throughout. The diamond quilting pattern is exquisitely worked and gives a vitality and cohesion that make this a stunning piece.

The variations of the popular Irish Chain pattern – Single, Double, and Triple – differ by having one, three, or five rows of small squares forming a chain that meets and crosses a similar chain running in the opposite direction at regular intervals. The design is constructed from two different blocks, one intricately pieced from small squares and the other either a plain larger square or a simple pieced block on which elaborate quilting or even appliqué patterns can be worked.

The squares that make the chain are usually all the same size, but occasionally a highly effective example is found in which the squares where the chains meet and cross each other are larger than the ones in the diagonal parts of the chain.

The most popular, and certainly the most graphic, historical examples of Irish Chain quilts are made from two colors, probably most often red and white, followed by blue and white. While the fabrics are generally solid colors, many beautiful quilts are made from mixtures of printed fabrics of the same tones, such as the blue-and-white examples shown here and on page 106.

There are also numerous highly effective versions that are made from multicolored scraps; and while the background is traditionally plain white or cream,

BLUE-AND-WHITE DOUBLE IRISH CHAIN

1880–1890

This quilt came into the collection as an unfinished top. Pat put it together and Meta Youngblood quilted it about 100 years after it was pieced. All the fabrics are prints or geometrics, including the background, which is assembled from a variety of creams, with patterns of pale red, black, brown, or blue. A large range of blues has been used for the chains and arranged in a random way. The squares in the middle pieced border are also random scraps.

a number of the examples in the collection show backgrounds that are mainly white with a small pattern. Checks, plaids, and prints all work well, depending on how they contrast with the background color.

Blocks are usually set square, which means that the chain runs through square or rectangular quilts on the diagonal. Sometimes, though, the blocks are put on point, which creates a squared, gridlike chain that can also be very effective.

Irish Chain quilts have been known since the eighteenth century and were popular in the American colonies as well as the British Isles. The pattern was taken west with the pioneers as they left the East Coast and settled in the Midwest. In her 1935 book, *The Romance of the Patchwork Quilt in America*, Carrie A. Hall relates the story of the furnishing of Nurse Hall at Mercy Hospital, a medical facility in Kansas City that operated as a free institution to care for paraplegic children whose parents could not afford to pay. The founder, Dr. Katherine Richardson, remembered the Irish Chain quilts used in the house where she grew up, and she launched an appeal for Irish Chain quilts to decorate the rooms in the nurses' residence and make them more homelike. Groups of women throughout the United

RED, WHITE, AND BLUE DOUBLE IRISH CHAIN

c. 1900

The red chain in this quilt is constructed from a tiny checked fabric in various shades of red, sometimes almost pink. There are a number of different blues, mostly navy with small-scale white designs. The large squares of the background and the outer border are made from a black-on-white print, while the white squares of the chain have a small pink pattern. The large blocks are quilted with a traditional rose design.

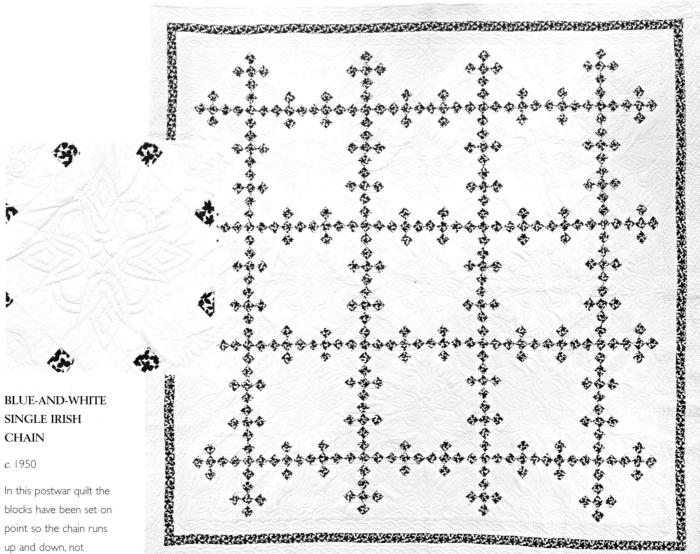

BLUE-AND-WHITE SINGLE IRISH CHAIN

c. 1950

In this postwar quilt the blocks have been set on point so the chain runs up and down, not across. The strong navy stands out even though there is a fairly high proportion of white in the pattern. The blocks are Double Nine-Patches alternating with plain white squares. The large plain white squares are quilted with a tulip square design, and a flattened version of the tulip is worked in each of the plain white Double Nine-Patch blocks. Both borders have been quilted with a cable.

States, who had organized Mercy Hospital clubs to show their admiration for Dr. Richardson and her work, swung into action. No less than 150 Irish Chain quilts, blue and white to echo the color of the nurses' uniforms, were hand stitched, beautifully quilted, and donated to the hospital.

SINGLE IRISH CHAIN

Perhaps the pattern's main appeal lies in its strongly geometric layout, which can be simplicity itself or show astonishing complexity of color and intricacy. The most basic of chains is probably the Nine-Patch Chain, in which Nine-Patch blocks are alternated with plain, unpieced blocks of the same color as the background of the chain blocks; but a simple Single Irish Chain can also be based on Five-Patch blocks,

which are squares of two colors made from five times five rows, again alternated with plain squares.

DOUBLE IRISH CHAIN

To construct a Double Irish Chain quilt, you need two or three colors of fabric. The background fabric will be for the plain blocks, with the chain contrasting strongly. If three colors are used, the chain will be constructed from two of them, and these should be different enough to make the chain stand out.

The plain blocks are also pieced, but are much simpler than the chain blocks. They can be made from a simple square of background fabric with border strips made from the background but with small squares of the contrasting fabric at each corner. When these two types of block are alternated, the double chain appears. The project block at the end of this chapter is a good example of the pattern.

TRIPLE IRISH CHAIN

The Triple Irish Chain pattern is traditionally – and most easily – pieced from two different Five-Patch blocks using two or three colors. However, if the center of the plain block is pieced as a standard Five-Patch block, it has so many seams that it becomes difficult to quilt, so various methods are used to add pieced border strips to plain squares to leave an open area on which to quilt.

BORDERS

Many historical examples of Irish Chain quilts have either no borders or very simple ones. Plain straight borders that may also act as binding are more common than elaborate ones, but there are beautiful quilts with pieced borders, most of them based on patterns made from simple squares.

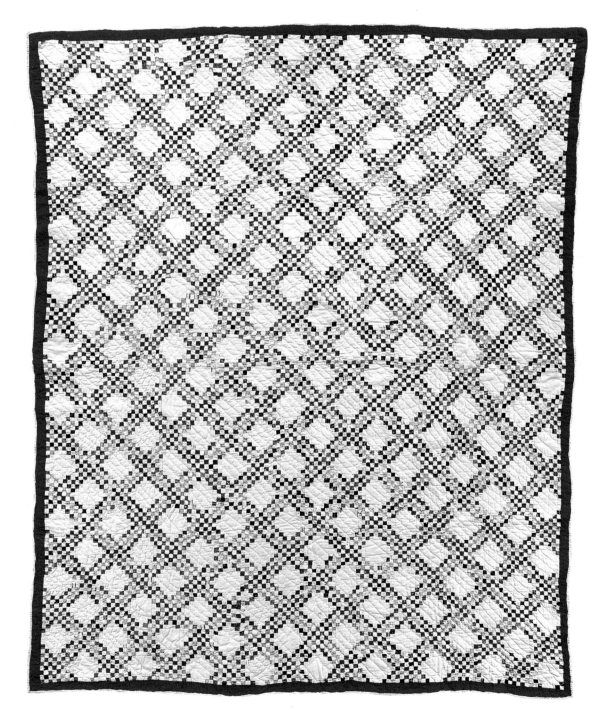

POSTAGE-STAMP TRIPLE IRISH CHAIN

c. 1875

Before it came into the collection, this quilt had been displayed nailed over a fireplace. Though incredibly greasy, sticky, and grimy, it cleaned up beautifully and is one of the prized pieces in the collection. It is a pure scrap quilt. Prints and geometrics have been mixed with solids in a gloriously random assortment. The squares in the chain are a mere ½ inch (1.2 cm) and the larger plain squares only 2½ inches (6 cm) each. The quilting is utilitarian at best – the diagonal lines are anything but straight.

PROJECT: IRISH CHAIN
SPEED PIECING

RED-AND-WHITE TRIPLE IRISH CHAIN

c. 1920

This modern-looking, highly graphic red-and-white quilt is a wonderful example of "less is more." This is not a scrap quilt — the same red and white fabrics have been used throughout, indicating that the maker bought them specially to make the quilt. The workmanship is of a very high standard: even without the advantages of using rotary equipment, the squares are square and the corners match superbly. The quilting consists of a simple horizontal and vertical grid covering the entire piece, including the borders, which enhances the quilt's bold, square elements.

This deceptively simple-looking quilt is made, like most Irish Chain quilts, from two different pieced blocks that are alternated throughout the quilt to create the diagonal chain effect. The design is put together from strips of red and white fabrics, which are sewn into strip sets and then cut into pieced units of various configurations that are reassembled to make the two main blocks. Although the piecing is fairly straightforward, it is easy to put the elements together in the wrong order, so check each stage before you actually stitch the seam. Seam allowances are ¼-inch (5 mm) throughout.

MATERIALS FOR ONE BLOCK

½ yard (0.5 m) of white fabric

•

⅜ yard (0.35 m) of red fabric

•

Thread to match

1 Cut 2-inch- (5 cm) wide strips from the red fabric and the white fabric.

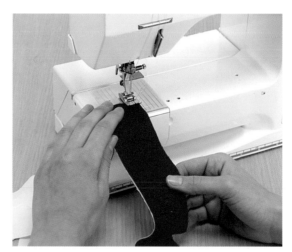

2 Sew five strips together to make a pieced strip set (set 1) of white/red/white/red/white.

3 Sew five strips together to make another pieced strip (set 2) of red/white/red/white/red. Press the seams for both sets toward the red fabric.

4 Cut each pieced strip set into 2-inch (5 cm) units across the seams, as shown.

5 Sew these pieced units together – set 1/2/1/2/1 – to make a checkerboard square.

6 Cut a 5-inch- (12.5 cm) wide strip of white fabric and sew a 2-inch- (5 cm) wide strip of red to each side. Press the seams toward the red fabric.

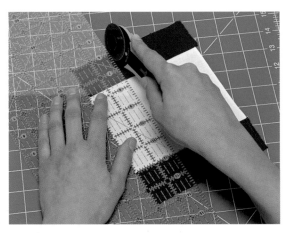

7 Cut two 2-inch (5 cm) strips from the strip made in step 6 for each checkerboard block.

8 Sew one strip to opposite sides of the checkerboard square made in step 5.

Inset: The result is a rectangle.

9 Using the remainder of the strip made in step 6, sew a 2-inch- (5 cm) wide strip of white fabric next to the red fabric on each side and press the seams toward the red fabric.

10 Cut two 2-inch- (5 cm) wide strips from the pieced strip made in step 9 to add to the checkerboard block.

11 Sew these pieced strips to opposite sides of the rectangular block made in step 8.

12 Cut a white rectangle to measure 8 x 11 inches (20 x 28 cm). Then cut two white strips to measure 2 x 8 inches (5 x 20 cm) for each block.

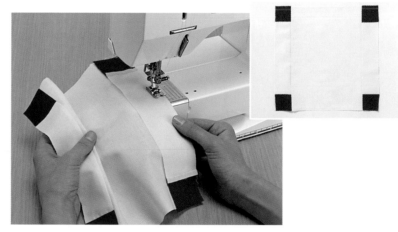

13 Cut four 2-inch (5 cm) squares from the red fabric and sew one to each end of the white strips cut in step 12. Press the seams toward the red fabric.

14 Sew one of these pieced strips to each long side of the white rectangle cut in step 12, and press the seams. Sew the large pieced squares (shown in inset) together in alternating order. Combining the two types of block this way creates the overall diagonal chain pattern.

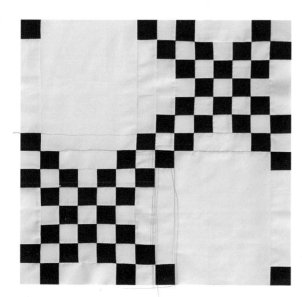

FINISHED BLOCKS

TRIANGLES

Of all the shapes for making patchwork patterns, triangles are among the ones most often used. Because they come in a variety of types, they can be combined in myriad ways to create complex, and complicated, designs; and when they are incorporated into patterns with squares, rectangles, and diamonds, they add enormously to the possibilities available to the quiltmaker.

DOUBLE FLYING GEESE

c. 1930

This quilt is a quintessential 1930s scrap quilt, made from several thousand separate triangles. Three right-angle triangles, made from different scraps and with their points alternating up and down, are joined into a strip, and two smaller right-angle triangles, all of them white, are added at either end to make each "goose" unit. Rows of strips point in the same direction up and down the quilt, and each strip is separated by other strips that are composed of white squares alternating with strips composed of four goose units. The plain white spacer blocks are filled with crosshatch quilting, and each goose triangle is quilted very close to the seam. This quilt has a very different feel from the one on page 116, which is also a Double Flying Geese piece.

BLUE-AND-WHITE OCEAN WAVES

1875–1900

Several different dark blue fabrics, all with close-set dotted patterns, have been used to make the blocks, giving this stunning quilt great vitality.

The types of triangles found most frequently in patchwork are the right-angle, or 90-degree, triangle, made most easily by cutting a square across the diagonal, and the equilateral triangle, which has three 60-degree angles and three sides of equal length.

Any triangle can be tricky to stitch, since by its very nature it must contain at least one seam cut on the bias. In some irregular versions none of the three edges is cut along the straight grain. Irregular triangular shapes are, however, used most often in crazy patchwork and are seldom seen in regular patterns.

When they are used, it is advisable to cut from a template and stitch employing the foundation-piecing method shown on page 137 for accuracy.

The other main type of triangle is the isosceles, in which two sides are the same length and two angles are the same, while the size of the third angle varies according to the length of the sides. Such triangles can be used effectively in patchwork, but are seen less often.

Two triangles – right-angle or equilateral – can be combined along one side to make a useful diamond shape. You will also find that if six equilateral

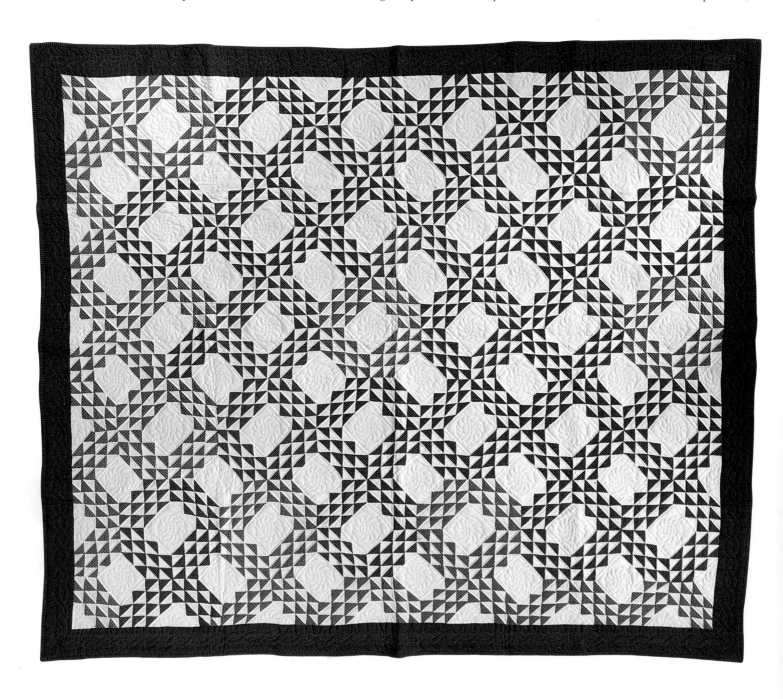

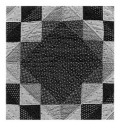

MULTICOLOR OCEAN WAVES

c. 1875

Made by a Pennsylvania Dutch quilter, this stunning quilt positively glows with excitement. The carefully chosen and organized fabrics are prints, not solids, so the maker was almost certainly not strict Amish, but the quilt was made in an area of Pennsylvania where there is a strong quilting tradition among both the Amish and the rest of the population. The quilt, never used, was supposedly one of a pair of trousseau bedcovers, but only this one is in the collection.

Although it is the same pattern and was made at about the same time as the quilt opposite, it is very different with its dark spacer blocks and border; bright, strong primary triangles balancing the more subdued rows; and pinwheel arrangements at the intersections.

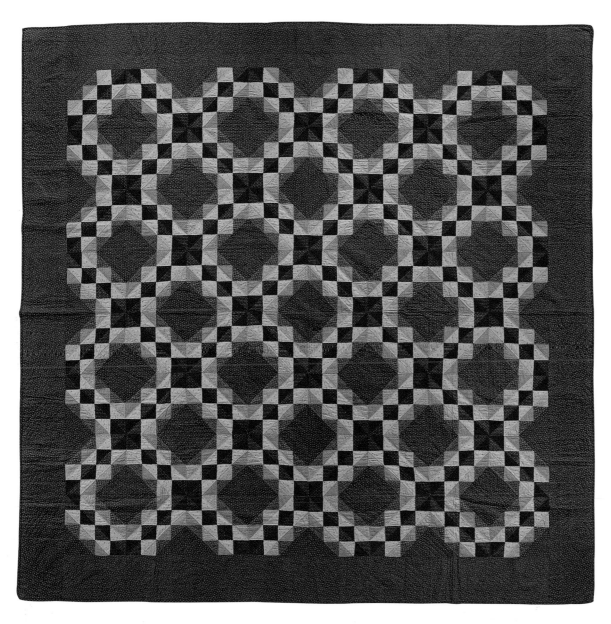

triangles are put together, they make an interesting pieced hexagon. This design can go anywhere that an unpieced hexagon might be used.

Many star patterns depend on triangles to create the points of each star (see Chapter 8), while both the handles and the bodies of various basket designs (see Chapter 10) and a number of tree patterns employ triangles to great effect. Border strips pieced from triangular shapes not only use up leftover fabric, but also add life and sparkle to a huge range of quilts.

RIGHT-ANGLE TRIANGLES

A vast number of traditional patchwork patterns incorporate right-angle triangles in their makeup,

which makes them relatively easy to stitch by machine. Such triangles are simple to cut – a square cut on the straight grain can be either cut and stitched along the diagonal bias, or stitched and then cut using the method for making pieced squares shown on pages 99–101.

This technique has become a popular way of chain-piecing large numbers of similar patches for making myriad patchwork designs. The patterns range from relatively simple ones such as Pinwheel, Ohio Star, Friendship Star, Maple Leaf, and Shoofly to more intricate ones like Ocean Waves, Birds in the Air, Flock of Birds, Crossroads, Delectable Mountain, and Lady of the Lake. (The latter pattern was named for a poem by Sir Walter Scott; it was

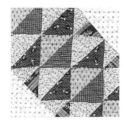

DOUBLE FLYING GEESE

c. 1875

This quilt uses the same pattern as the one shown on pages 112–113, yet the result is very different. The colors are more subtle and the juxtaposition of light and dark more invigorating. The rows of geese are arranged diagonally instead of up and down, resulting in a totally different dynamic effect. The fabrics are typical of their period, and a fairly wide selection, especially of darker ones, is used to make the triangles. The central area of each strip shows the same creamy yellow – except in the lower right-hand corner. Here, two strips point in opposite directions and create an almost shocking change of pace. Pink is the pre-dominant color in one of them, and the beige centers of the other are made not from triangles but from squares. The dark shading of the strip is moved to the outer edges.

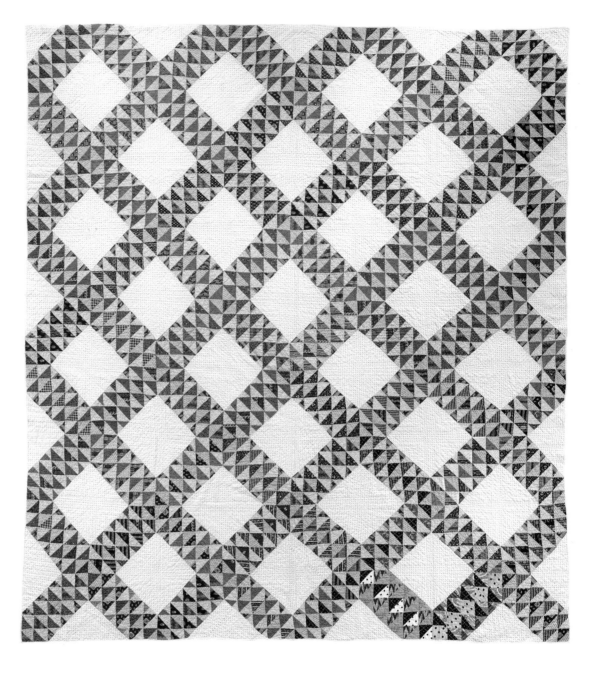

set in the Scottish Highlands, from which many American pioneers came.)

The Flying Geese design, widely used for borders and found in Amish Bars and Strippy quilts, is based on right-angle triangles. Units are made by joining a smaller right-angle triangle to each straight-grain side of a larger version, and these pieced units are joined so that the point of the larger triangle meets the base of the larger triangle in the next unit. Strips of Flying Geese can be combined, with or without sashing, to make whole quilts. Most of the so-called "frame" quilts, in which a central "medallion" square is bordered by a series of pieced borders – a type of

quilt that was extremely popular in the early to mid-eighteenth century and is still made today – had at least one border of Flying Geese, presumably to show off the maker's skill. A variation of the pattern is Double Flying Geese, in which each unit is made up of five triangular pieces instead of three.

Snowball patterns can be created by stitching a small right-angle triangle over each corner of a large square, which turns the square into an octagon (with uneven sides). Many popular leaf, flower, and tree designs, from Tree of Life and Pine Tree to tulips and Maple Leaf, are based on configurations of right-angle triangles. The sawtooth or feathered edge

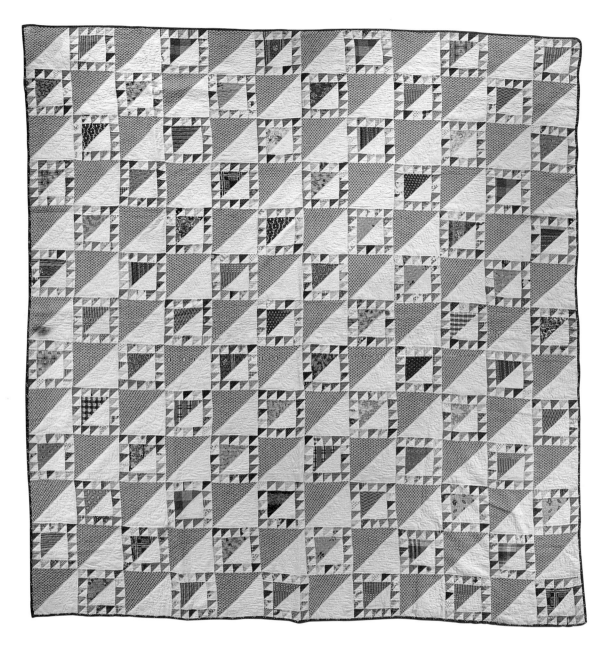

LADY OF THE LAKE

c. 1865

The seller's tag on this beautiful variation of the traditional Lady of the Lake design identifies it as Rocky Glen, but that pattern has a sawtooth edge around only two sides, not four as found in the Lady of the Lake block. Here, the Lady of the Lake blocks appear to be made from random scraps with only the white fabric consistent throughout, and they are alternated with squares made from two large contrasting white and light brown right-angle triangles. The use of a number of different red fabrics gives a sparkle to the piece.

found in many beautiful and elaborate patterns, often stars, uses right-angle triangles that alternate in light and dark fashion to make a broken outline around the shape, and a similar jagged effect can be achieved by using right-angle triangles to make the handles in a number of basket patterns.

EQUILATERAL AND ISOSCELES TRIANGLES

Equilateral and isosceles triangles, unlike their right-angled cousins, cannot be cut with more than one edge along the straight grain (and it is a good idea to make sure that this one edge is always straight). Because at least two of the edges will be cut across the grain, slightly off the true bias, the patterns made from either type are sometimes pieced by hand using the so-called English paper-piecing method, rather than by machine. This technique gives very accurate seams, but because it is time-consuming, it has lost favor in the fast-paced world of rotary-cut and speed-pieced quiltmaking – which is a shame, since there are a number of fascinating patterns that can be created to show these shapes at their best advantage.

One of the most familiar of these designs, which can be made using either equilateral or isosceles triangles, is called Thousand Pyramids. In it, rows of identical triangular shapes are turned one up, one down, with the colors alternating between light and dark or shaded in some way to create, accurately, fabulous mosaic patterns of great beauty.

Equilateral and isosceles triangles can both be cut using rotary equipment, and it is also possible to use the foundation method to piece some designs.

FABRICS AND COLORS

As always in patchwork, the choice of fabric and color is fundamental to the overall effect and the finished effort. Most of the triangles found in patchwork patterns are small and many of the designs are busy, so they lend themselves to using scraps, although patterns that are constructed from chain-pieced right-angle triangles (see the method on pages 162–167) will require squares that are large enough to work with. Making blocks for a quilt using the hand paper-piecing method (see pages 137–139) gives those who like sewing by hand the opportunity to keep a portable project on the go, and it can help make inroads into an abundant scrap basket.

TREE OF PARADISE

1930–1940

This pattern has a number of names – Tree of Life, Christmas Tree, Pine Tree – but Marie Webster, in her book *Quilts, Their Story and How to Make Them*, shows a virtually identical tree design that she has called Tree of Paradise. The arrangement of the triangular "leaves" into contrasting lights and darks is handled masterfully, with an overall effect of liveliness and vivacity. The bright green of the trunks does not appear to have faded over the past decades.

BABY BUNTING

1930–1940

One of the most complicated of all triangle patterns is Baby Bunting, with its curves and sharply pointed isosceles shapes. In this busy example, held in check only by the white background, hundreds of scraps, including gingham, stripes, checks, and dotted patterns, plus a wealth of other printed designs, have been combined to make a colorful and lively quilt. The color placement appears to be totally random, with the curving pieces that separate the corner quarter circles from the jagged triangles joining up and snaking through each block with no plan but great élan. Considering the vast number of seams the quilter must contend with, the quilting itself is cleverly planned and fairly heavily stitched. The maker must have been an expert quilt-maker – the piecing is accurate and well done.

A number of the finest historical examples are based on a narrow range of color. Many beautiful Feathered Star quilts, for example, are made in white and a single other color, such as red or blue. Other designs work well in the more muted tones found in many of the quilts made before 1840, when shades of brown and pink were popular and accessible, and also in many of the quilts made in the latter half of the nineteenth century.

The contrast of light and dark is always crucial, so the overall value of a color, determined to a certain extent by the color next to it, is of utmost importance. Traditional designs can be refreshed by reversing the usual format of color on a white background and putting white or cream on a background of a single color, a variety of harmonizing shades, or a combination of the two. Black or dark blue or green backgrounds can be particularly striking.

PROJECT: TRIANGLES
FOUNDATION PIECING

WHEEL OF FORTUNE

c. 1940

The pinwheel in the center of each block is pieced from assorted scraps of typical 1930s and '40s fabrics, bright enough to hold their own against the zing of the turquoise and pink of the background. Most of the elements are outline-quilted, and the same utilitarian diamond cable pattern has been stitched on each of the three borders. The design is based on two different right-angle triangles that alternate to make the pinwheel.

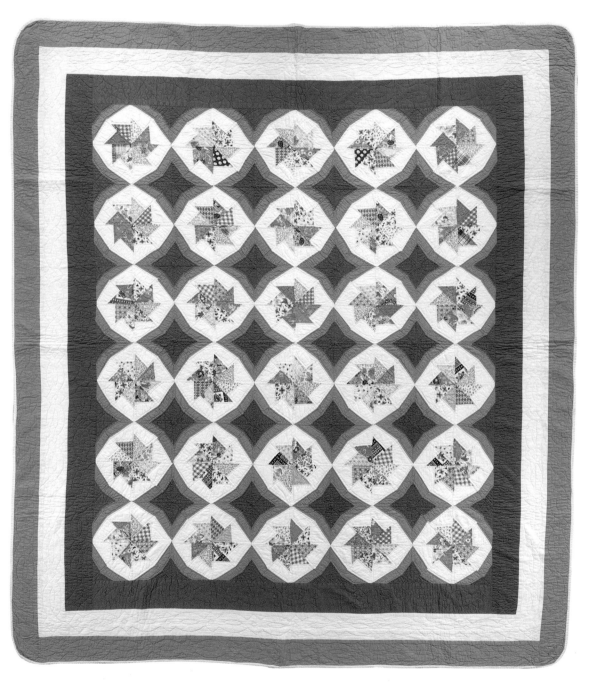

This pattern is based on two different right-angle triangles that form a flowerlike design when the pieced shapes are combined. We have used a foundation-piecing method, which allows piecing with a high degree of accuracy.

There are a number of ways to work foundation-pieced patchwork, and several choices of foundation. Lightweight interfacing marked with a pencil adds an extra layer to the finished shape, but makes it easy to check the position of each new piece of fabric before it is sewn. Lightweight muslin (calico) is an alternative, but the piece will be thicker. Paper foundations must be stitched using a tight machine stitch, so you can remove the paper.

MATERIALS FOR ONE BLOCK

¼ yard (25 cm) of lightweight interfacing or other foundation material

•

Scraps of 8 different fabrics, each about 6 inches (15 cm) square

•

1 piece of turquoise fabric, 8 inches (20 cm) square

•

1 fat eighth (9 × 22 inches) each of pink and white fabric

•

Thread to match

It is possible to cut shapes from templates. However, cutting roughly and trimming the excess after stitching, though using a bit more fabric, makes positioning easier. Check the position of each newly stitched piece before trimming the allowances to a scant ¼ inch (5 mm), then press. Positioning can be tricky, because foundation piecing is worked in reverse. The pattern, including the numbers indicating the stitching sequence, is drawn on one side of the foundation, and fabrics are placed on the other side, right sides together. The seam is stitched from the right side of the foundation and each fabric is flipped over in sequence and pressed before the next one is added.

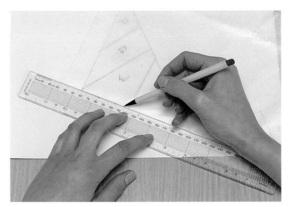

1 Trace the patterns onto your foundation material, adding a ¼-inch (5 mm) seam allowance around all the edges. You will need four A and four B foundations for every block.

2 Make a template for shape 1 and cut eight fabric triangles, adding a ½ inch (1 cm) seam allowance. We have used eight different 1930s repro fabrics, but the design is also effective using only one or two fabrics. Cut eight 4- × 6-inch (10 × 15 cm) rectangles from white fabric.

3 Place a patterned triangle right side up on the wrong side of a foundation for shape 1. Check that you have a generous seam allowance around all three sides and pin it in position.

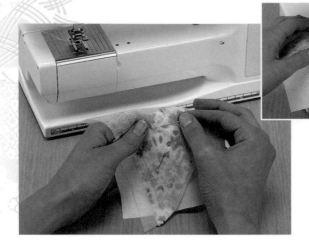

4 Place a white rectangle right side down on the patterned triangle. Check all positioning very carefully. *Inset:* Stitch the seam to join the two pieces.

5 Turn the white piece to the right side and press. Trim the seam allowance if necessary.

6 Cut eight 3- x 6- inch (7.5 x 15 cm) rectangles of turquoise fabric for each block. Place one long straight edge of a turquoise shape along the stitching line between the turquoise and white shapes. Make sure it is facing in the right direction and leave a seam allowance. Check all positioning very carefully.

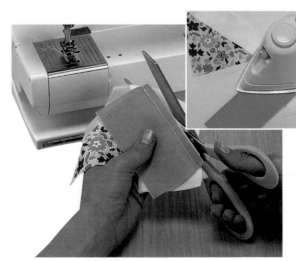

7 Starting at the point of the main foundation triangle, stitch the seam between the turquoise and white pieces, working toward the base.

8 Trim the turquoise and white fabrics along the seam, leaving a scant ¼-inch (5 mm) allowance. *Inset:* Turn the turquoise shape to the right side and press.

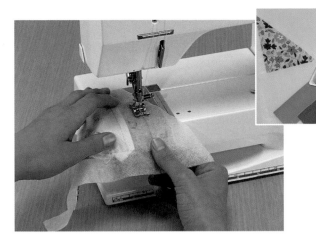

9 Cut eight 3- x 5- inch (7.5 x 12.5 cm) rectangles of pink fabric for each block. Place one long straight edge of a pink piece along the final seam line.

10 Stitch the seam starting at the side edge of the main triangle and working toward the base. *Inset:* Press the seam.

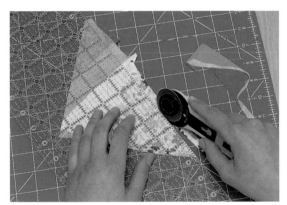

11 Trim this final seam allowance. Repeat to make three more large pieced triangles the same size from pattern A. Use pattern B to make four large triangles of that design, which looks similar but is slightly different.

12 Place each pieced triangle right side down on a cutting mat. Use a rotary cutter and ruler to trim them evenly, leaving a ¼-inch (5 mm) allowance outside the marked edge of the foundation on all three sides.

13 Decide on a color sequence and join the trimmed triangles in alternating pairs. *Inset:* The pink and turquoise sections will be mirror images of each other. Join the resulting squares into a Four-Patch block.

FINISHED BLOCK

PATTERNS

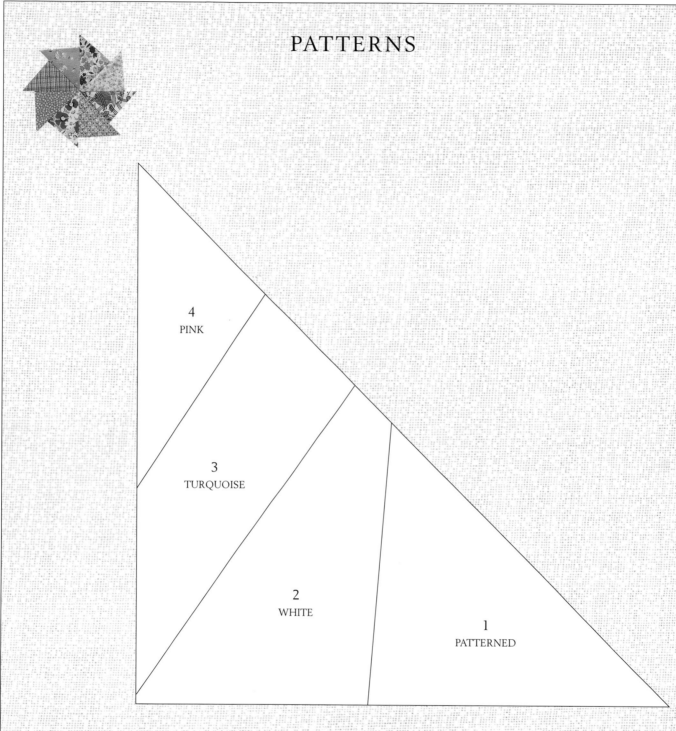

4
PINK

3
TURQUOISE

2
WHITE

1
PATTERNED

PATTERN A

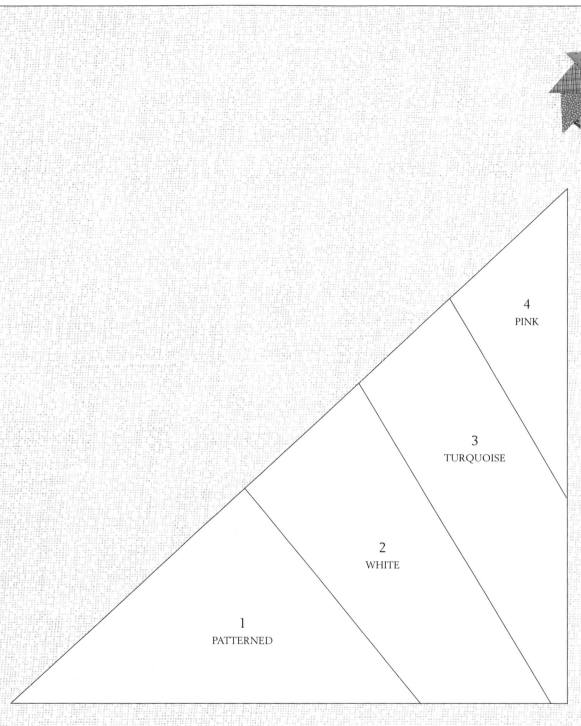

PATTERN B

TRIANGLES

The patterns are deceptive. They look the same at first glance, but are different. Mark foundations carefully to avoid confusion. The right-angle triangles that make the patterned piece in each triangle are the same size, but are oriented differently. The patterns shown are the finished size. Add a ¼-inch (5 mm) seam allowance to the fabric when cutting out.

STARS

While there may not be as many star patterns used on quilts as there are twinkling bodies in the heavens, there are probably more motifs based on stars than on any other type of design. Stars appear in patchwork block designs and as appliqué motifs, and they are used in many different forms for quilting. Most sampler quilts contain at least one star block, and variations of star patterns can be combined to make a star sampler. Because the pieces used to make star designs are generally small, many of the most beautiful historical examples of star quilts were pieced from scraps.

OHIO STAR

c. 1875

This fine example of a star quilt is very, very scrappy, with most of the blocks made from at least four different fabrics. However, the consistency of tone and value is superb, and the placement of each piece seems to be carefully considered, even in the "superstition" block (two down, four across). Setting the blocks on point gives a lively, vigorous feel to a simple but effective piece of work.

Eight-pointed stars, such as Evening Star, can also be pieced as Four-Patch and Double Four-Patch blocks, again using squares and right-angle triangles. The intriguingly named Tippecanoe and Tyler Too is a complicated arrangement, in which the star's points are visually blunted by contrasting triangles in each corner of the block. The pattern name dates from 1840. William Henry Harrison, a general who had led a defeat of the Shawnee tribe in 1811, was nicknamed "Old Tippecanoe," after the place where the battle took place. When he ran for president as the Whig party candidate in 1840, having been defeated by Martin Van Buren four years earlier, John Tyler was chosen as his running mate, and the slogan was coined. The campaign is remembered as

an undignified circus, and "Tippecanoe and Tyler Too" became a catchphrase. As a footnote to this little history lesson, Harrison, who was 68 when he was elected, was the oldest man to take office until Ronald Reagan was elected nearly a century and a half later. He was also the first to die in office, from pneumonia, only a month after his inauguration, having served the shortest term in history. His illness developed from a chill suffered after he went outdoors on a bitterly cold day. He was succeeded by Tyler, and the slogan became part of American culture, aided and abetted by Whig quilters who made the pattern avidly.

Harrison's successor as Whig candidate in the next election – 1844 – was Henry Clay, a renowned

VARIABLE STAR

_1860–1870_

Every block but one (a superstition block?) has been pieced from a single chosen fabric and set on point to contrast with dark green spacer blocks that are typical of the mid-nineteenth century. The rows of star blocks are color-coordinated diagonally across the quilt, except in one row towards the right side. All of the fabrics in the border except the red print have been used in the blocks. Simple crosshatching has been used to quilt the blocks, with a large triple cable over the borders.

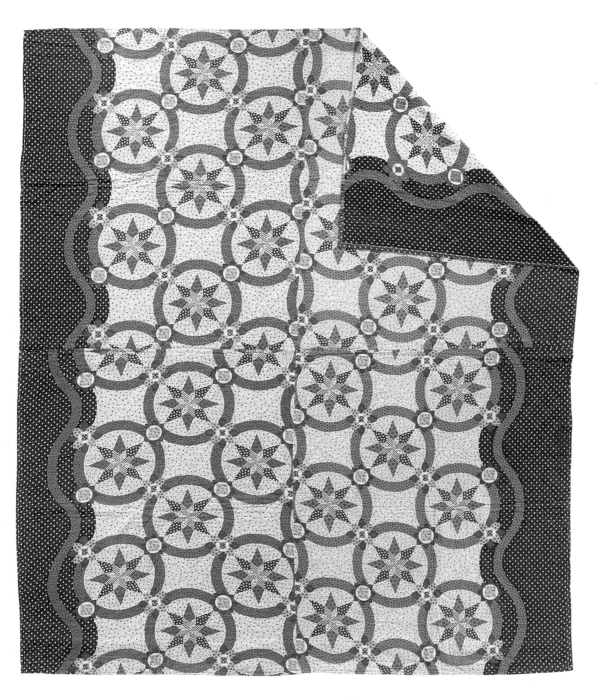

STAR COVERLET

c. 1930

This is the quintessential bedcover made from feed sacks. Four large sacks, printed with a double eight-pointed star pattern, have been stitched together to make each side. One side is blue, the other red, and they have been quilted together with a simple grid through a very thin batting (wadding). The borders are part of the design of the sacks, and the maker seems to have tried to match the designs as closely as possible, given the constraints of her materials. This is a fascinating historical document, completely of its time in the depths of the Great Depression, when everything was hoarded and reused, even the bags in which the farmer bought his animal feed and his wife her flour and sugar.

statesman and senator from Kentucky. Clay's Choice, another popular star pattern of the mid-nineteenth century, which was made as a Double Four-Patch with a four-pointed diamond-shaped star, was named in his honor. It had several other names, including Harry's Star and Henry of the West.

DIAMOND STARS

Stars can also be made from 45-degree diamonds, which fit together to create the eight points. The lovely scrap quilt that forms the basis for the project in this chapter is such an eight-pointed star, as are both of the Lone Star quilts (pages 128 and 129) featured. For some, the simple eight-pointed star is easier to piece by hand because of its set-in seams, although the larger versions can be assembled as strips which are then cut at 45-degree angles and pieced in rows of alternating color.

The name most often associated with a simple eight-pointed star is the LeMoyne Star, named for Pierre and Jean-Baptiste LeMoyne, or LeMoine, French brothers who settled in the Louisiana

STAR OF THE EAST

c. 1875

This six-pointed star uses the method for Lone Star. A number of patterns are used; the colors are fairly consistent and the contrast between the dark inner and outer rows and the lighter middle one is strong.

independence, was incorporated into the state flag, and into quilting folklore.

The pattern serves as an example of how names change according to location. This design was widely made at about the same time in Pennsylvania, where it was known as Star of Bethlehem, and in Missouri, where quilters dubbed it Star of the East.

A more complicated version of Lone Star is Broken Star, or Carpenter's Wheel. Squares of contrasting, usually plain, fabric are added between each point of the large star, and concentric rows of diamonds radiate around the edges (see page 129).

SIX-POINTED STARS

Six-pointed stars can be drafted using a drawing compass. The resulting 60-degree diamonds are joined in a similar way to that used for eight-pointed

stars, and the patterns can be combined with hexagons and equilateral triangles to create some of the most beautiful of all mosaic designs.

MARINER'S COMPASS

The most complex pieced star patterns are known as Mariner's Compass. The elaborate, time-consuming design is characterized by concentric rings of sharply

SEVEN SISTERS

c. 1875

Another six-pointed star pattern from Oklahoma was made in the same era as the quilt opposite. It uses many of the same color combinations, but the placement of the blocks is more random. A traditional mosaic design, it is based on combining interlocking diamonds of the same size throughout to create a hexagon shape with a six-pointed star in the center, surrounded by six more stars, all contained within another, larger hexagon. Viewed in one way, the pink triangular spacer blocks create an even larger star shape around the hexagon. The closely worked quilting is a diamond crosshatch pattern.

pointed starbursts that radiate out from a central circle. Each layer of points is usually made from a different fabric to contrast with the rows next to it, and because the points are generally very sharp, the piecing must be done extremely carefully. The only Mariner's Compass quilt in the Patricia Cox collection is a splendid blue-and-white example. The quilt is shown on page 1.

APPLIQUÉD AND QUILTED STARS

Numerous appliqué star patterns also exist, such as the nursery-type five-pointed star, which is very difficult to piece since it is not a standard geometric shape. Small versions of stars of any shape are easier to apply to a background than they are to piece.

Stars of any size and shape can be used for quilting patterns, and are found on quilts of all sizes and ages.

PROJECT: EIGHT-POINTED STARS
HAND PAPER PIECING

LEMOYNE STAR

c. 1875

The simple scrappy stars used in this quilt are worked in an interesting mixture of fabrics. Some are made from a single fabric cut carefully to create an interesting secondary pattern (bottom right-hand corner); others are balanced blocks made from only one print or two positioned with symmetry. Some are combinations of three or four fabrics joined seemingly at random, as in the detail above.

This version of an eight-pointed star lends itself to hand piecing with the so-called English method, used also for hexagons, in which the pieces of fabric are basted to a backing paper of the finished size and shape before being joined by whipstitching them together. This block uses three different templates to make the square: the 45-degree diamonds that comprise the star itself, the corner squares, and the fill-in triangles between the points in the center of each edge. It is fun to cut the fabric diamonds in ways that create secondary patterns when the stars are joined.

MATERIALS

¼ yard (25 cm) of cream fabric for the background

•

¼ yard (25 cm) of print fabric for the star

•

¼ yard (25 cm) of green fabric for alternate block

•

Cardstock (backing) paper for foundation

•

Template plastic

•

Thread to match

1 Trace and cut out templates for each shape from the patterns on page 139. Use them to cut foundation (backing) papers. For each block, you will need eight diamonds, four triangles, and four squares.

2 Draw around each template on the wrong side of the fabric and cut out the shapes, adding a seam allowance of approximately ¼ inch (5 mm). We have cut ours in a way that will give a circular pattern in the center of the finished star.

3 Pin each fabric piece with its wrong side to a foundation (backing) paper and baste the edges under, keeping the knots on the right side of the fabric.

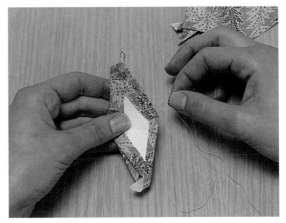

4 Join the diamonds in pairs and then combine to form an eight-pointed star, whipstitching (over-sewing) them together right on the edges of the shapes.

FANS AND OTHER CURVES

Sinuous curves give a design a lively sense of movement that cannot be achieved by straight lines. Because curves have a reputation for being difficult, however, many stitchers avoid them. Curves are used in appliqué work more often than in patchwork, but for those who prefer to piece their blocks, many beautiful patterns exist, from fan-shaped designs and the circular patterns known as plates to Double Wedding Ring and the versatile block called Drunkard's Path. The chapters dealing with appliqué patterns contain many fine examples of applied curves. All the quilts shown on the pages of this chapter are patchwork and can be pieced by hand or, in some cases, by machine.

FANCY DRESDEN PLATE

c. 1930

The multicolored fans on these "fancy" plates are made from an enormous number of different scraps, most of them floral prints entirely typical of their era. The segments have rounded ends, while the yellow pieces that occur at the compass-point positions, all made from the same fabric, are pointed. The top is heavily marked, and there may have been some delay between when the top was made and when the quilting was worked.

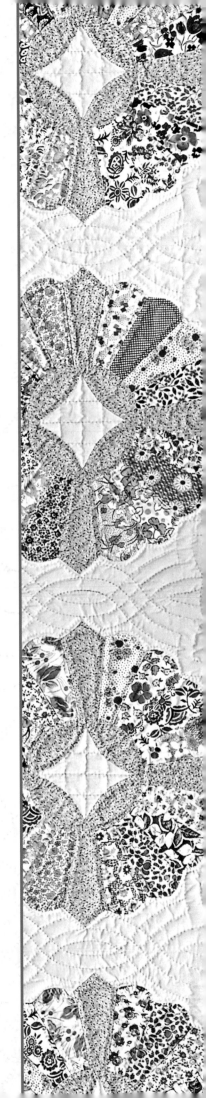

Optical curves can be made from straight lines, such as when thick and thin strips are joined to make the rounded edges of the pattern in Asymmetrical Log Cabin and in Log Cabin Hearts. Another example is the use of tiny squares that blend and contrast color values and trick the eye into seeing curves, or larger squares with the corners cut off to make octagonal shapes that look round. Still, there is immense satisfaction in the visual quality of a curve that really is curved.

The quarter-circle pattern, known most often as Grandmother's Fan or in Victorian times as Fanny's Fan, is highly versatile. Fan-shaped sections with blades made from a variety of fabrics can be set in the corners of plain background blocks, which can then be arranged in a number of ways to create paths, rings, or lines. The fans can all point the same way or face in alternate directions. If fan blocks are set on point, the fan pattern is upright and the quilt has a very different feel from one in which the blocks are set square.

LOVE RING

c. 1940

This variation of the fan pattern is entirely typical of its time, from the completely random use of its multicolored scraps to the overall bright pastel coloring. The Love Ring setting is also found in Drunkard's Path quilts. The quilting is beautifully planned and executed using a mixture of straight and flowing lines. The pink triangles in the ice-cream-cone border echo the base of the fans, and the pale green print binding gives a gentle edge to the piece.

SUNFLOWER

1930–1940

This Dresden Plate variation has curved "petals" made, as with so many quilts of this type, of random scraps. Some of the scraps are floral, but a lot of them are stripes, checks, and even plaids that appear to be shirt material. Many of the colors have faded, but the quilt retains a lively effect akin to pinwheels whirling in the wind. The center of each flower is appliquéd in place, and the ice-cream-cone border with its bright pink binding displays the same random choice of scraps — again, some of them faded — as the flowers themselves.

Adding a strip of sashing between fan blocks and positioning the fans with the corners facing each other creates a pattern called Wagon Wheel. Alternating two plain blocks with two fan blocks, points facing, makes a passably realistic Butterfly pattern. Fans can be arranged into a number of traditional patterns that create secondary straight-line patterns across the quilt, with names such as Love Ring, Chain Links, Diagonal Wave, and Snake in the Hollow.

Fan patterns are based on a quarter circle that is appliquéd or joined to a background block. The blades can have flat, rounded, or pointed ends, and there is usually a smaller quarter circle in the corner to create a base, or handle, for the fan shape. The blades can be joined by hand or by machine. They can be appliquéd to a full square of background fabric, or, alternatively, a curved seam can be cut in the background to reduce the bulk behind the fan.

DRESDEN PLATE

c. 1930

This bright-colored countrified quilt was purchased in Alfred, Maine. Like the others of its type in this chapter, it is made from a large selection of randomly placed scraps typical of the era, but two things set it apart. The first is the somewhat unusual use of sashing (with the addition of corner squares); the second is the highly decorated pieced border on three sides, which is made from half-plates. The plates are appliquéd to the background squares, so the centers are part of the background, not appliquéd as they are on the quilt on the previous page.

PLATES

Plate patterns can be created in a similar way as fans, but are full circles that are usually appliquéd to the center of a background block. The best-known design is called Dresden Plate. As with fans, the segments can have rounded ends, or they can be flat or pointed, and many versions have a mixture of some or all of the possible combinations. Blocks are generally combined side by side and row on row in a straightforward way, but some quilts have

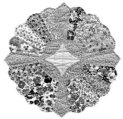

c. 1930

The wonderful ice-cream-cone border on this Fancy Dresden Plate quilt is worked in scraps of the same type as those used to make the plates. The pastel colors, while bright, would pale somewhat without the yellow used for the sections in the center of each block and the binding. The exquisitely stitched quilting, which echoes the shape of the yellow pieces, makes this a truly stunning example of the quilt-maker's art. A detail of this quilt is shown on pages 140–141.

Because the segments that make up both fans and plates are small, the patterns lend themselves to using scraps, and backgrounds are usually plain, most often white or cream. Dresden Plate blocks that are joined edge to edge have relatively large, plain background areas, and many examples are heavily, and beautifully, quilted in these spaces.

RINGS

Of all the patterns made up of rings, the best-known is probably Double Wedding Ring. There are many versions of this design, which was at the height of its popularity in the 1920s and '30s, when numerous patterns with templates were published in magazines and newspapers, and a good number of precut kits were available, too. Also, like fans and plates, the rings in many versions of Double Wedding Ring are made up of small pieces, so the scrap bag provides an excellent resource for many quiltmakers. Perhaps this fact explains at least partly why such an intricate (some would say difficult) pattern was so widely made in the Great Depression, when times were hard and so much other, more pressing work presumably needed to be done.

The origin of the name Double Wedding Ring, which was attached to a few earlier, but different,

sashing and even corner squares between blocks. For some reason, the borders found on many Dresden Plate quilts are fairly fancy, ranging from half-plates that match the ones in the quilt to ice-cream cones to appliqué circles.

quilt patterns, remains obscure. Quilts have been made by hopeful maidens and for blushing brides for most of their recorded history, but there are few examples of this particular pattern before the end of the nineteenth century. A design with rings fashioned from triangular shapes occurs in the pattern known both as Pickle Dish and as Indian Wedding Ring. Perhaps the name of the similar, but less complex, Double Wedding Ring originated here.

Another Indian Wedding Ring design, also called Single Wedding Ring, is based on octagonal shapes surrounded by dark and light triangles. It appears to be an older pattern. Unlike Double Wedding Ring, it is most effective when only two colors are used.

COMBINING CURVES AND TRIANGLES

A number of highly intricate patterns employing curves and triangles to make blocks developed in the nineteenth century. They are complex to work, but the results can be stunning. One of these, dating from the 1840s, is often known as New York Beauty, but according to the New England Quilt Museum

DOUBLE WEDDING RING

c. 1930

This wonderful quilt top was purchased in Edina, Minnesota. It was made in the 1930s and backed and quilted by Meta Youngblood, working to a motif designed and marked by Patricia Cox, about 60 years later. The 12-part rings are anything but typical, and pieced with great care. The tiny pieces are random scraps of Depression-era fabrics, and the new binding fabric was chosen to match as nearly as possible the pink in the connecting squares. The quilting consists of a close-worked diagonal grid with a rose in the center of each large space.

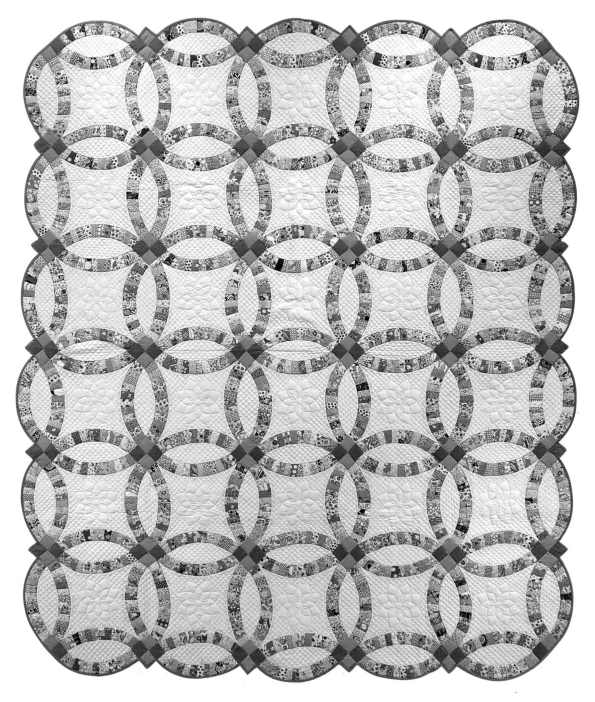

SINGLE WEDDING RING

c. 1915

Although the names seem to be related, this is a very different kind of quilt from the one opposite. Its curves are optical trickery, created by the blue octagonal center of each Five-Patch block. When one looks at a single block, the squared-off shape is obvious, but the illusion created by the whole quilt is that shapes are curved. Each block is separated from its neighbors by plain sashing made from the same fabric as the background and quilted with large diamonds in both directions. The blue fabrics are all solids, but there are several shades used. The triangles in the border are the same size as the ones in the blocks. Note that none of the corners of the border match, and that three are finished with diamonds, a shape that doesn't occur elsewhere in the piece.

in Lowell, Massachusetts, most of the surviving examples were made not in New York but in the South, and the pattern has no less than 25 names, from Polk in the White House, to Crown of Thorns, Rocky Mountains, and Sunrise. Mohawk Trail is another curve-and-triangle block. It is made as a Double Four-Patch, with fan shapes in one corner of each patch alternated to twist and turn themselves into the finished block. These patterns tend to work best as high-contrast two-color quilts.

ROBBING PETER TO PAY PAUL

The name Robbing Peter to Pay Paul is applied to a large variety of curved patterns that rely for their effectiveness on the contrast created when dark and light values are alternated in positive and negative form on two simple shapes. Complex and interesting versions can be made using more than two colors, but most examples contain only two. The stronger the color contrast, the more effective the design.

Perhaps the best-known version is Drunkard's Path. Despite its name, which is objectionable to some, and its curves, which can be tricky to piece, this pattern has remained popular since the middle of the nineteenth century, when it was sometimes used in so-called Temperance quilts of blue and white. Its popularity did not stop there, however, and many examples exist with names like Fool's Puzzle, Snowball, World Without End, Falling Timbers, Dove, and Love Ring. Amish quilters, whose strict

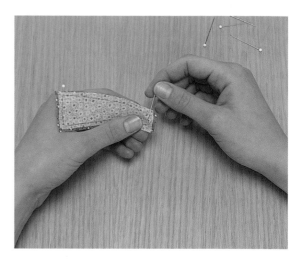

4 Mark the fan blades on the wrong side of the fabric and cut out eight for each block, leaving a ¼-inch (5 mm) seam allowance all around. You can mix and match the fabrics as you wish.

5 Pin the first two blade pieces together. Pin at the corners, just a single thread below the drawn line.

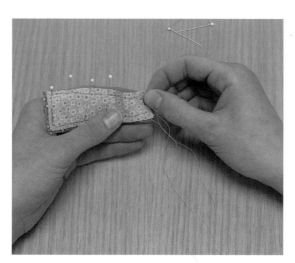

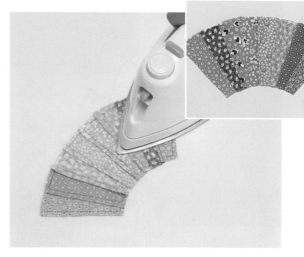

6 Use as few pins as possible along the rest of the line, and make sure you pin and stitch just below the drawn line on both sides. Join the pieces together using a running stitch.

7 Continue joining pieces until the fan shape has been completed. Press all the seams to one side.

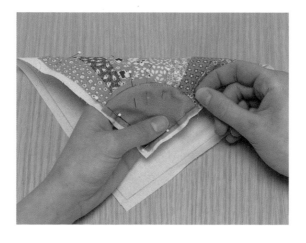

8 Slip the bottom raw edge of the fan under the quarter circle and pin along the curved line of the quarter circle. Blindstitch along the marked line through all the layers – quarter circle, fan, and background fabric.

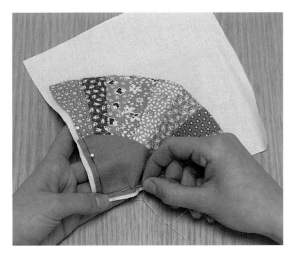

9 Use the large Fan Shape pattern on page 157 to mark the top stitching line of the fan. Pin, then blind-stitch the top edge in place, turning under as you work.

10 Baste the straight edges of the fan and the quarter circle to the background fabric outside the marked line to secure them. The raw edges of the motif do not quite reach the edges of the background, which reduces bulk when blocks are combined.

FINISHED BLOCK

BASKETS

In spite of being somewhat more complicated than some designs, Basket patterns are enduringly popular. Extremely versatile, they provide scope for enormous creativity on the part of the quiltmaker. Many traditional Basket patterns are patchwork, while a wealth of appliqué designs can give inspiration, and some of the most interesting and beautiful Basket quilts contain a combination of piecing and applied work. The designs can be simple or complex, the color combinations endless.

FRENCH BASKETS

1920–1930

French Baskets is a design by Marie Webster (1859–1956), an early quiltmaker, designer, and author of the first full-length history of quilting. This delicate design has been worked in three layers. The blue background blocks have been appliquéd to the large white background and the baskets appliquéd through both layers. The handles are bias strips that intertwine under and over each other.

PROJECT: CAKESTAND
SPEED PIECING

CAKESTAND

1875

This vibrant quilt was made by Minnie (or Manda) Myer, an Englishwoman who traveled via the Outer Banks and made her way through the Cumberland Gap to Richmond, Indiana. The traditional pattern has been beautifully worked to make a quilt of simplicity and freshness that belies its age with a thoroughly modern look. The acid green fabric, widely used in the latter half of the nineteenth century, is a difficult color to match in today's fabrics.

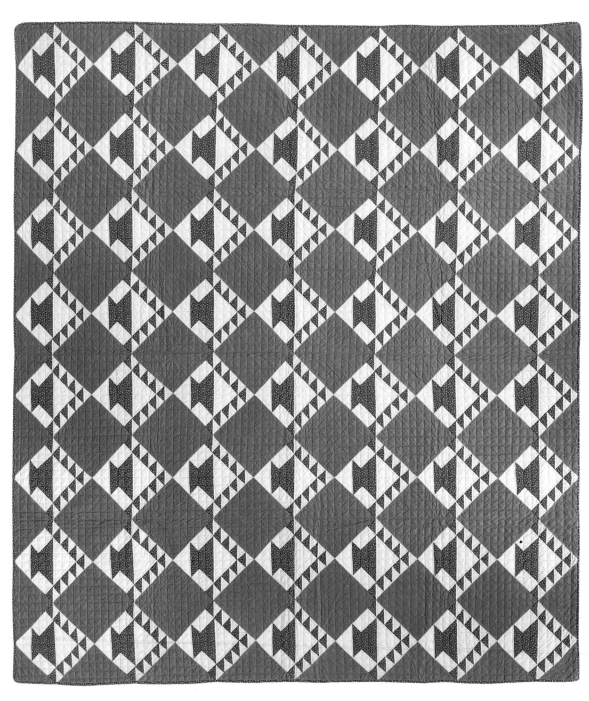

The Cakestand pattern can be made entirely from triangles. The method used to construct the triangle squares in this pattern is similar to that used in the Four-Patch Hourglass block (see pages 98–101). Because you are cutting across the hypotenuse of the triangle, you must cut a square larger than the size of the finished one, plus ¼-inch (5 mm) seam allowance. In this pattern each square is cut once, so you add ⅞ inch (2 cm) – i.e., a 1½-inch (3.8 cm) finished square plus ⅞-inch (2 cm) allowance equals a 2⅜-inch (5.8 cm) cut square.

MATERIALS FOR ONE BLOCK

9 × 22 inches (23 × 56 cm) of green fabric

•

9 × 22 inches (23 × 56 cm) of ivory fabric

•

1 piece of pink fabric for setting squares,
8 inches (20 cm) square

•

Thread to match

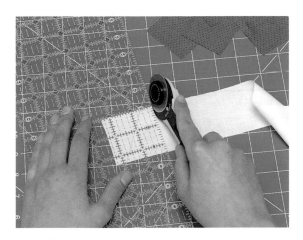

1 The basket handles are made from half-square triangles. Cut one 2⅜-inch (5.8 cm) strip from green fabric and one from ivory. Then cut 2⅜-inch (5.8 cm) squares from each fabric. Nine squares will give enough triangles to make two blocks.

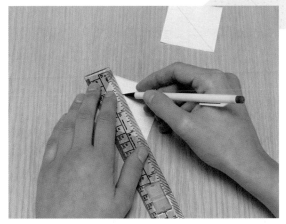

2 On the wrong side of each ivory square, use a pencil to mark a diagonal line from corner to corner in one direction only.

3 Make two piles of squares and place one ivory square right side down on one green square. Stitch a ¼-inch (5 mm) seam along one side of the marked diagonal line, chain piecing to make the required number.

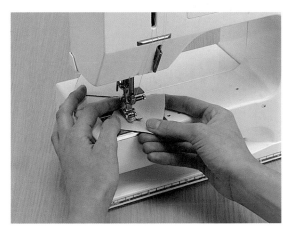

4 Repeat to stitch along the other side of the diagonal line, chain piecing as in step 3.

HEXAGONS

The hexagon, with its six sides, is one of the most familiar and widely used of all geometric shapes, and it was one of the earliest designs to be used in quiltmaking. British examples date from before 1800, and it was popular in the United States throughout the nineteenth century, when it was known as Honeycomb or Mosaic.

GRANDMOTHER'S FLOWER GARDEN VARIATION

c. 1930

The yellow flower centers are surrounded by rings of plain hexagons which are in turn bordered by flower prints typical of the 1930s. Each rosette is outlined in white and joined to its neighbor by a row of small green diamonds that make a path through the quilt. Equilateral triangles are used at the points of each rosette, and the entire piece is bordered with diamonds cut in half along their length and bound in the same green fabric.

5 Add another light-colored hexagon next to the first one. Stitch it to the center hexagon.

6 Continue adding light hexagons to the center. *Inset:* Stitch the hexagons along their adjoining seams to make a rosette.

7 Add a light hexagon in the same way to opposite sides of the rosette to create the elongated shape.

8 Add a row of dark hexagons around the elongated rosette in the same way. Choose a thread color to match the dark fabric.

9 Using thread to match the cream fabric, add a row of cream-colored hexagons to the elongated rosette in the same way. Don't forget to add the two at the ends.

10 Starting in the center, remove the basting threads. *Inset:* Remove the backing papers. The finished block can be combined with other blocks in the same way as you assembled the first one.

FINISHED BLOCK

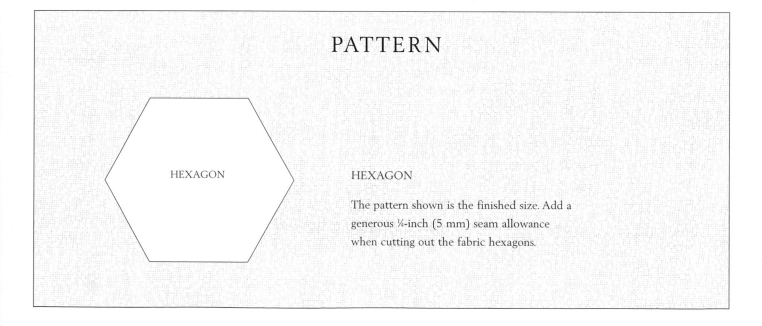

PATTERN

HEXAGON

HEXAGON

The pattern shown is the finished size. Add a generous ¼-inch (5 mm) seam allowance when cutting out the fabric hexagons.

CRAZY QUILTS

Crazy quilts, associated with genteel ladies in Victorian England, were also made in huge numbers in the towns and cities of North America. The women were eager to show off their skills in embroidery, which decorates most of the crazy quilts of the era, as well as the expensive fabrics used, frequently scraps from their fine silk, velvet, and even woolen dresses. There are a good number of crazy quilts in the Patricia Cox collection. Because they are made from fine fabrics like silk and velvet, many of them are too fragile to travel to be photographed, but the ones shown here are among Patricia Cox's favorites.

HEXAGON LOG CABIN CRAZY QUILT

c. 1890

This exquisite quilt is so controlled that it is a "crazy" only by virtue of the beautifully decorated hexagon blocks set between stars made from diamond-shaped Log Cabin pieces. The embroidery is worked to a very high standard, especially the myriad flowers.

istorians presume that the piecing methods used to make crazy quilts were employed long before the Victorian era, but because such patchworks would have been put together from any available scraps, and presumably received heavy use, few survive. The crazy quilt as we know it is a High Victorian invention, made for show and to advertise the maker's skill with a needle. These quilts were often made as throws or lap quilts, or used as bed or table covers, and since they were subjected to limited use, many have survived more or less intact.

The idea was to use scraps of any shape, stitch them together at random, square off the resulting patchwork, and embellish it with embroidery. There are numerous examples of crazy quilts made of cotton and wool, especially in the United States, but the most prized versions are made from beautiful silk and velvet fabric scraps, many of which were left over from dressmaking projects.

SILK AND WOOL CRAZY QUILT

1891

This beautiful quilt not only is dated but also is initialed "I.M.B." It is made from hundreds of wool scraps, the majority of which are narrow strips that have been stitched around a central panel, which is embroidered with the same skill shown in the heavily decorative stitching covering the entire quilt. The motifs include birds (as in the detail above) and other animals, leaves and flowers, people, and a "good luck" horseshoe.

VELVET AND SILK CRAZY QUILT

1884

The rich, subdued coloring of this piece is only one of the elements that lift it out of the ordinary. Many of the scraps are patterned and figured velvet and silk brocade, and a number of the embroideries, such as the bulldog and the owl in the top left corner, are machine-made and applied, perhaps dress decorations. The blades of the open Chinese fan in the square with the horse and peacock are made of narrow ribbons stitched together to make the shape. The fan theme is continued onto the dark maroon velvet border with a row of connected motifs embroidered to form an inner border. The date, 1884, was marked in the second block from the top left-hand corner but was never stitched.

Most were mounted on a backing of muslin (calico), which strengthened the delicate fabrics and provides an additional reason as to why so many are still in good condition more than a century later.

EMBROIDERY

The embroidery is a strong element in a crazy quilt. The seams between pieces are usually covered and decorated with a variety of stitches, and countless motifs are used to embellish suitable spaces on a quilt. Flowers, fruit, and leaves are among the most popular designs, with animals, especially birds, and people often featured. Fans of various types, and horseshoes, are also widely used; in fact, most crazy quilts contain at least one fan, or an owl, or a horse-shoe, if not all three of these motifs. Many of the quilts are dated, and quite a few of them are either signed or monogrammed.

PROJECT: CRAZY PATCHWORK
STITCH-AND-FLIP PIECING

CONTROLLED
CRAZY QUILT
c. 1890

Hexagonal units have
been constructed from
scraps of cotton and
combined in a crazy
fashion. The pieced
shapes are then
trimmed to size and
joined to yellow squares
that produce a gridlike
structure in the midst
of the whirling patterns
made by the red, blue,
brown, beige, and black
fabrics. Among a number
of unusual features of
this quilt are its organ-
ized nature and the total
absence of embroidery.

The most familiar form of the crazy quilt is a large piece composed totally of random scraps, however, many of the most interesting crazy quilts were made from blocks that were squared off and then combined in a grid.

This method of making contained or organized crazy quilts was particularly popular in the United States, and Pat Cox's collection has a fair number of such examples. Making crazy quilts in blocks provides a way of controlling the chaos inherent in the style, and the patterns that result can be quite fascinating. In this quilt, for example, the yellow squares impose a grid on what would otherwise be a random arrangement of fabrics.

MATERIALS FOR ONE BLOCK

Large selection of scraps of cotton fabric

•

4-inch (10 cm) square of yellow fabric

•

Template plastic

•

Thread

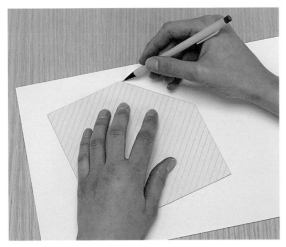

1 Using the pattern on page 187, make a template for the hexagon shape. The pattern is the finished size with no seam allowances. The seam allowances are added in step 10.

2 Gather up a pile of scraps and try out various colors, or put a selection of scraps in a bag and pull them out at random.

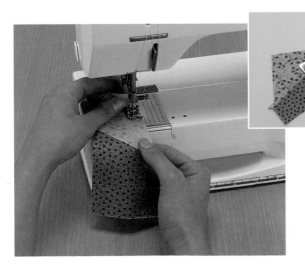

3 The scraps will be stitched together one by one to form a rough hexagon shape, with a generous seam allowance all around the outside edges of the shape. Start with the middle section, and join the first two fabrics, with right sides together.
Inset: Press the seam.

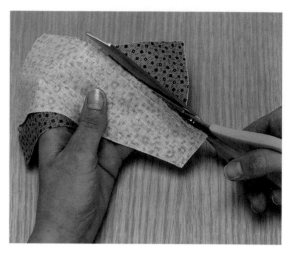

4 Stitch the third fabric to the previous two and then press. This method of construction is sometimes referred to as "stitch and flip."

5 Because many of the pieces will overhang the work, trim the seam allowances as necessary.

6 Where necessary, join two short pieces to make a larger one. *Inset:* Press the seam.

7 Add the joined piece from step 6 to one end of the middle section and press.

8 Add the final piece and press again. You can check the size using the hexagon template.

9 Place the stitched shape right side down on a cutting mat and position the template on it.

10 Using a rotary cutter and ruler, trim around the template, leaving a ¼-inch (5 mm) seam allowance on all six sides.

11 Repeat to make three more units. You can, if you wish, make a large string-pieced block and cut the hexagons from it.

12 To make the center square, cut a 4-inch (10 cm) square of yellow fabric.

13 Join one side of each hexagon to the yellow square. Stitch two opposite sides first and press the seams open. Then stitch the other two sides, starting and finishing on the seam lines of the two previously joined hexagons. Press the seams open.

14 Stitch the remaining seams to join the hexagon together to make the finished block.

FINISHED BLOCK

PATTERN

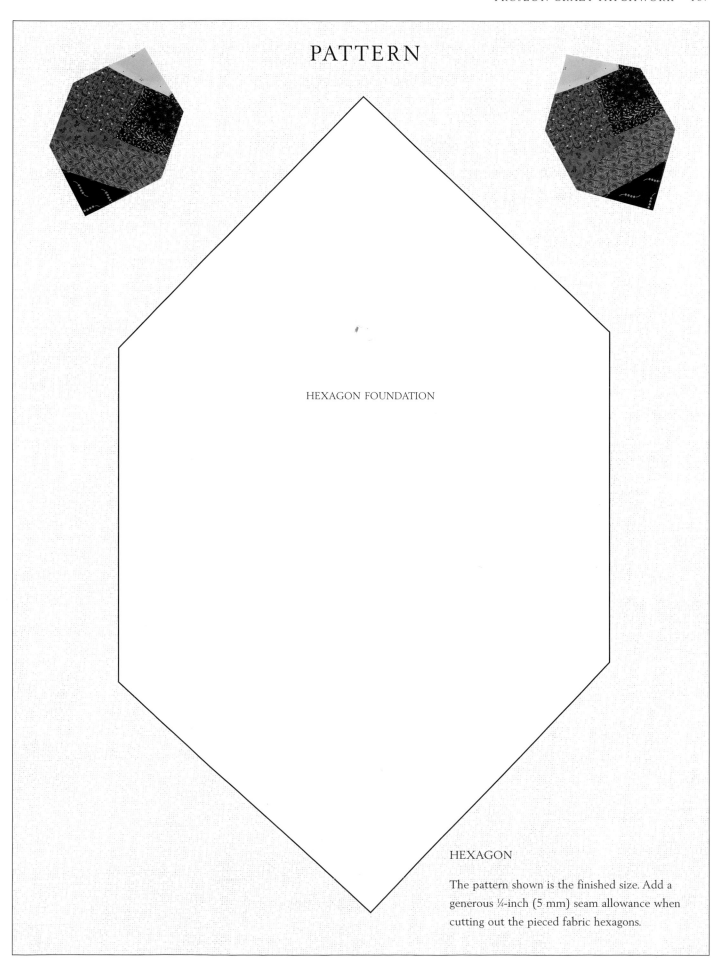

HEXAGON FOUNDATION

HEXAGON

The pattern shown is the finished size. Add a generous ¼-inch (5 mm) seam allowance when cutting out the pieced fabric hexagons.

LOOKING AFTER QUILTS

There are quite a number of issues to take into consideration when collecting quilts. This section offers guidelines on how to choose quilts to buy, whether or not to attempt to clean and repair antique quilts, whether, when buying unfinished quilt blocks, to finish them or not, and also how to store your quilt collection to preserve the delicate material.

When she started acquiring quilts, Pat bought, almost at random, things that she liked and that appealed to her strongly. As she added more and more pieces to her collection, she began to specialize in several areas and to develop her own guidelines (see box).

If you come into possession of a quilt that is not in pristine condition, it is important to decide how far to take remedial work to preserve the piece for a while longer. Some people consider remedial work to be a negative thing. A repaired quilt can be seen to have lost its unique characteristics and also its historical significance. Whatever your view on restoring quilts, any cleaning or repairing you choose to do should be undertaken only after seeking advice from someone experienced in such matters.

Even quite a small quilt collection can take up a lot of space in your home. Quilts are very susceptible to environmental damage, so it is crucial to store them safely.

The quilts featured in this section have all been repaired in some way. Think carefully about any restoration work before you begin, so the quilts can be preserved for posterity.

ACQUIRING QUILTS

- Ask yourself: Is the price right for the quality of the quilt?

- Do not buy a quilt with the idea of selling to make money. This RARELY happens.

- Have guidelines as to what you are looking for: for instance, a certain pattern, an unusual quilting design, a historical period you want an example of, scrap quilts, kit quilts, pieced quilts, examples of specific patchwork patterns, or appliqué quilts.

- Specialize in a certain style, period, or color combination.

- Unless you have unlimited resources, you need to stay within a budget. The quilt has to say something to you. Do not buy anything and everything.

- Buy quilt tops or sets of blocks only if you particularly like them, or if you know they will otherwise be destroyed. Do not buy them with the idea that you will finish them, unless you are certain you are being realistic about this.

- If a quilt really speaks to you and you can afford it, buy it. You will have many more regrets about the ones you didn't buy than about the ones you did.

MILDEW AND MOLD

When Pat found this fine example of a red-and-green pre-Civil War quilt featuring one of the most popular mid-nineteenth-century patterns, it had a large area of mildew right through the middle (detail below). Such a problem could not be left untreated if Pat bought the quilt, but there was no guarantee that the stain could be removed.

A strong bath of lemon juice and uniodized salt, together with a spell in the sun, seemed the best option to try. When the green fabric turned blue under the treatment, Pat thought she had ruined the quilt. But when it was finally washed clean, the green color returned, the blue disappeared, and the stain, though still visible in a few places, most notably in the middle of the left-hand side of the quilt, had almost vanished. More important, the damage had been arrested and the quilt was saved from rapid deterioration.

Such treatment should be attempted *only* on cotton fabric. Bear in mind that you should always get expert advice before attempting to clean any old quilt.

TO FINISH OR NOT TO FINISH

Pat often buys quilt tops and sets of blocks from unfinished quilts. She feels that, if time and finances allow, it is better to turn these treasures into finished quilts than to leave them to deteriorate, and the collection is dotted with good examples of this stewardship.

Conservators and experts disagree about whether collectors should alter or finish an old quilt. Some experts regard such work as permissible only if old fabrics, preferably from precisely the same period as the original quilt, are used, while others see it as unwarranted

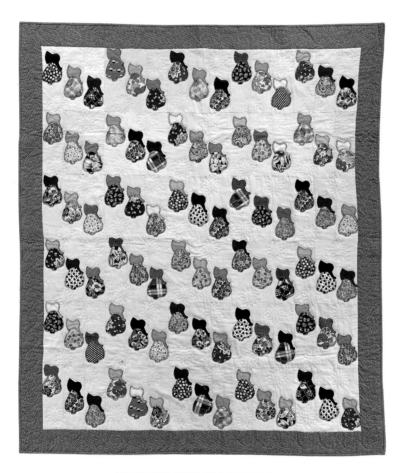

SUNBONNET SUE TRIPLETS
c. 1930

These unusual babies came into Pat's hands as a set of blocks. Charming though they are, their maker had not been too careful about the size of the background squares or the precise placement of the appliqués on them – each figure is on a separate strip of fabric and the blocks were joined as sets of three staggered strips – and the process of fitting the blocks together in a way that made a pleasing and balanced quilt turned into something of a challenge. Pat and her daughter Joan spent many hours working them into the lively result, which was then machine quilted to stabilize and enhance it for future generations to enjoy.

KALEIDOSCOPE STARS
c. 1875

When Pat bought this quilt top, it was sashed in the bright green fabric and yellow corner squares shown in the inset. The garish color did nothing to enhance the string-pieced stars with their myriad fabrics, which were mainly in shades of red and blue, so she separated the blocks, removed the old sashing, and added the complementary dark blue solid-colored sashing with corner squares in a similar value of red. Pat does not generally use vintage fabrics when finishing an old top. Here, she used a new cotton fabric of the same type in the quilt. The heavily worked quilting is done by hand and is in keeping with the date of the original blocks.

interference. Pat, however, believes that because finishing a top or a set of blocks adds many years to its expected life span by stabilizing the fabrics and making the quilt usable to give pleasure to its new keeper, it is justified, provided the work is done carefully and sympathetically and with fabrics compatible with the original in color and pattern.

If you are in doubt about the advisability of repairing damage to an old quilt, try to find an expert to assess it before you take any steps. Many museums and some educational institutions have departments of textile conservation, and it is worth contacting local auction houses and antique dealers, who may be able to point you in the right direction. Sensitive repairs can make a piece more beautiful, make it usable, and also prolong the life of a quilt. By the same token, badly done restoration work can affect the look of a piece adversely. It can also lower its market value, and worse still, damage the quilt even more. Get professional advice before you act.

SCHERENSCHNITTE
1900–1920

When this quilt came into the collection, several of these red-and-white "paper-cut" appliqués were badly in need of repair, which Pat carried out so well that only an expert would be able to spot them. The poorly matched border pattern is offset by the beautiful diagonal grid quilting, which is more recent than the appliqué work.

CARING FOR YOUR QUILTS

- Do not store dirty quilts.

- *Never* store quilts in a plastic bag or box.

- Use old, well-washed pillowcases or sheets to wrap quilts in.

- Do not store quilts in cedar chests or near unfinished wood. There is oil in the wood that can stain them.

- If possible, roll each quilt separately. If you do not have room to roll and have to fold them, change the way they are folded every few months. Fabric tends to break down along folded edges.

- Be sure to store quilts in a clean, dry area that is free from insects. Use moth crystals if you are keeping wool quilts in a storage area.

- Place fragile quilts – crazy quilts, silks, etc. – on a bed and spread them out, one on top of another, with no folds. Cover the top one with a clean sheet.

- Do not store quilts in direct or artificial light.

- Do not stack too many quilts on top of one another.

- The ideal storage method, if you have space, is to fold the quilt carefully, placing acid-free paper in all the folds, and put it in an acid-free box.

- Washing a quilt successfully and without damage depends on a variety of things, and should be done carefully. There are so many variables that you may need guidance in the methods used. Always seek advice before taking any action unless you are absolutely sure about what you are doing.

INDEX